victor sen yung's
great wok cookbook

victor sen yung's

great wok cookbook

illustrations by karen mcbride

ECHO POINT
PUBLISHING

Victor Sen Yung's Great Wok Cookbook
by Victor Sen Yung

Published by Echo Point Publishing
Brattleboro, Vermont
www.EchoPointBooks.com

All rights reserved.
Neither this work nor any portions
thereof may be reproduced, stored in a
retrieval system, or transmitted in any capacity
without written permission from the publisher.

Copyright © 1974, 2021 by Victor Sen Yung

Victor Sen Yung's Great Wok Cookbook
ISBN: 978-1-64837-022-9 (casebound)
978-1-64837-023-6 (paperback)

Illustrations by Karen McBride

Cover design by Kaitlyn Whitaker

Cover photo by Africa Studios, courtesy of Shutterstock

To my father, Sen Gam Yung

acknowledgments

May I take this occasion to thank Mr. Dan Kibbie, friend and producer of "The Virginia Graham show," who first suggested that I write this book and then worked diligently to "keep me on schedule" until the book was completed. My thanks to Mary Kibbie, who performed the tedious and exacting chore of typing the original manuscript; to my sister and brother-in-law, Mr. and Mrs. Bing Chin, who worked many, many hours with me on the recipes; to Karen McBride, whose imaginative and artistic talent created the drawings and the diagrams and Jan Kubota who contributed the calligraphy. For their editorial help, I extend my thanks as well to Sylvia Cross and to the staff of Nash Publishing, whose critical advice and suggestions helped so much to guide me in this, my first venture into writing.

contents

Introduction *3*
Chinese Foods *11*
Utensils and Food Preparation *33*
Rice *41*
Egg Rolls and Won Ton *47*
Appetizers *55*
Soups *73*
Eggs *103*
Pork *113*
Chicken *141*
Beef *163*
Vegetables *187*
Seafood *195*
Noodles *205*
Index *213*

victor sen yung's great wok cookbook

introduction

Because I played Hop Sing, the Cartwright's irascible houseboy on NBC-TV's "Bonanza" series for fourteen years, it's not surprising that many people identify and associate me with cooking. Over the years, I have received letters from most of the eighty countries where the show airs asking me if I really can cook and if I have a favorite recipe or two to share. *The Great Wok Cookbook* is my humble way of answering both these questions.

During the course of my life, I have acquired an enormous appetite for, and interest in, Chinese cooking. Of course, when your mother and father are Chinese, it's easy to develop a taste for the delights of Chinese cookery!

San Francisco was the Chinese immigrants' Ellis Island, welcoming mostly young men, who came to the United States in the mid-1800s to work on the railroads and in the gold fields. Most of them didn't stay in the Bay City for more than a few days, but moved on to Sacramento, Marysville, China Camp and other little Western towns along the railroad right-of-way.

My father was among the thousands of young Chinese who came to *Gum San* (The Gold Mountain) to seek his fortune in the New World. The story of my family is not much different from that of millions of European families who came to America to improve their lot and the quality of their lives.

The Chinese workers who arrived during this building period of the West, were primarily from the province of Kwangtung, or Canton, China. They were of many diverse educational backgrounds, possessing many different skills, but the hardships, famines and economic instability of their homeland gave them good reason to come to America. These men weren't looking for fame; most of them came to make their fortunes. Hoping to return to China with the money they had saved from working as coolies and day laborers, they dreamed of taking care of their families and elders with the riches they would earn in the "white man's land."

Many of these men accomplished exactly what they had set out to do. The savings from their meager pay on the railroads, or the gleanings they took from the hard work they put in at some "played out" gold claim, made them big men back in China. Of course, the legend of their success spread and was exaggerated in the retelling. Before long, more and more young Chinese were squeezing into the steerage quarters of San Francisco-bound Yankee ships. For many, the Gold Mountain turned out to be a disappointment.

As the eighteenth century came to a close, the railroads were approaching completion and the gold mines were fast becoming barren. I've been told that approximately twenty or twenty-five thousand Chinese laborers were in this country at that time, most of whom found it difficult to compete in a white man's world where work had become scarce and the language was foreign. Many of the Chinese who had not been able to save their money, or those who had arrived after the labor market had dried up, were forced to take whatever kind of work they could get. Women were scarce in the West in those days and, before long, it became commonplace to see Chinese men doing women's work; they took positions as laundrymen, dishwashers, tailors, houseboys and cooks. Many turned to farming as independent growers, contract farmers, or farmhands. Some of them scraped together enough money to open small "kitchens" or cafés featuring Chinese home cooking or Chinese and American food.

As these kitchens, cafés, laundries and small businesses prospered through the diligence and hard work of their proprietors, the immigrants began to lose their interest in returning to China. Instead, they brought over their wives and children so that they too could take part in the "American dream." These laborers from Kwangtung

Introduction

were quick to see and take advantage of the educational opportunities that existed here for their children.

Communities with the larger concentrations of Chinese population began to open restaurants that catered to both the residents of Chinatown and to the general public. The Americans who ventured into these establishments not only grew to love Chinese food but also to identify themselves as friends, patrons and adopted members of the Chinese families that operated these restaurants.

Chop Suey became the popular trademark of Chinese food.

As these small groups of pioneers and workers followed the paths of the railroads south and east seeking new opportunities in new areas, the familiar signs, Hand Laundry and Chop Suey, began appearing in communities across the face of America. But chop suey was really an American stew cooked in the Chinese style, and had no real connection with the variety of precise ingredients that are a part of the richly authentic tradition of Chinese cuisine. White patrons who experimented and explored these authentic dishes soon began to appreciate the delights of real Chinese food, and demanded more and more of it.

Today, some of the finest Chinese restaurants are no longer identified as chop-suey houses; instead, they bear proud marquees such as Kan's, Golden Pavilion and the Four Seas in San Francisco; Ruby Foo's and Doriental in New York; Victor Lim's in Detroit; Lee's Canton Café in Chicago; and General Lee's, House of Kwong, Grand Star, and Far East Terrace in Southern California. Chinese food is accepted for quality, culinary excellence and service in these and other fine restaurants in this country. They are comparable to the finest dining establishments anywhere in the world.

As I mentioned earlier, the first Chinese who came to America— and those who followed them for many many years afterwards—were Cantonese. Thus the restaurants that sprang up and prospered here served only Cantonese food.

In the years following WW II, a number of Mandarin-style and Shanghai-style restaurants sprang up—and in more recent years, some popular Szechwan-style restaurants. I think it's important for you to know at this point that the basic techniques of Chinese cooking are essentially the same whether the style is from Peking, Shanghai, Canton, Szechwan or Hong Kong. Through the centuries, geographic and climatic differences have created variations as to ingredients and seasonings used to satisfy regional palates. But, the cooking techniques and methods of food preparation are still the same. Once you have mastered these basic techniques and methods, you will have little or no difficulty in enlarging your recipe repertoire to include almost any regional variation.

Down through the centuries, the unique style of food preparation developed by our ancestors became a basic and important part of Chinese culture. There was a time, in the not too distant past, when a Chinese meal was looked upon by most Americans as some sort of exotic magic from the mysterious East. I feel privileged to have seen those attitudes change dramatically in my lifetime. Today, Chinese food is an established part of our American scene. It is as welcome on the family menu as is Irish stew and Italian spaghetti. I believe that Chinese cookery has played an influential part in the American culinary heritage.

From my early youth, the time I spent first at the sink and later at the stove became an integral part of my daily life. In my family, learning to cook was not "women's work"; it was a way for each child to begin contributing and become involved in the total family picture.

At age twelve, the basic knowledge of cooking I had acquired at home became a desired qualification when I took a job as a houseboy in order to help finance my education. These "school jobs" were difficult to find and eagerly sought by the Chinese youngsters in San Francisco. I was fortunate enough to find a job serving a family on Nob Hill. So, cooking and kitchen work helped give me an early boost up the educational ladder. If I had known at age four, when my father first handed me a dish towel to dry the dishes, how much enjoyment and satisfaction kitchen work would provide me over the years, I might not have been so reluctant to begin. Of course, I had no way of knowing then that drying the dishes would lead to writing a book on Chinese cooking!

I hope that by reading and using this book you will find that Chinese cooking is really quite simple. There are basic techniques and methods that are easily mastered after just a little practice. There are condiments, seasonings and ingredients used in Chinese cooking that are fun to learn about and easy to obtain and use. There is pleasure and relaxation in planning and shopping for a meal in the Chinese manner. There is excitement and adventure in preparing the various dishes.

Chinese cooking involves a method or procedure of preparing foods that is economical, nutritious and palatable. It involves a

Introduction

method of cooking that retains and enriches natural food colors, making the foods unusually appetizing and delicious in a multitude of recipe variations. But most important, it involves a way of cooking that retains the natural vitamins and minerals so necessary for good health and well-being.

A little of "this" and a little of "that," thrown together, steamed, stir-fried, etc., is usually the way you get a Chinese recipe. Traditionally, Chinese chefs serve long periods of apprenticeship: from dishwasher, to vegetable man, to fry cook, to chef. During this long training period, recipes are committed to memory. The only problems then are selecting ingredients and bringing together the base seasonings to enhance the dish or give it an identity of its own.

The recipes in this book are meant to be used as guides for preparing specific Chinese dishes. With practice, your individual tastes or family preferences will cause you to alter some of the amounts and ingredients found herein. Before long, these cookbook recipes will reflect your own personal touch—with a pinch of this, a dash of that and a little more or less of "these and those."

The majority of Chinese dishes make very well-balanced meals served alone. They are concocted with varying combinations of meats and vegetables. One dish and a bowl of rice can make a nourishing meal for one person. The old cliché about eating a Chinese dinner and being hungry two hours later, does not hold true for the diner who eats his *rice*! The bland taste and the wonderful texture of steamed white rice are compatible and complementary to all Chinese dishes. Rice is enjoyed as the starch substitute for the bread and potatoes of American and European meals.

To generalize, Chinese meals are noteworthy for their *variety*. Not only the variety found in each meal, but the variety from meal to meal and day to day. This is possible because of the many ways of preparing and cooking basic ingredients and the seemingly endless combinations possible.

Starting with rice and soup—one dish should be enough for a meal for two persons, one more dish is added for each additional person dining. (For the beginner, it is advisable to prepare fewer dishes, but larger portions for larger groups; thus allowing for simpler preparation and less confusion.) For variety and balance, it is a general practice to add pork, beef, poultry or seafood dishes to the main soup and rice dish.

I have found that the primary attributes one can derive from learning to cook Chinese style, are patience and an appreciation of timing. The first step is to check your store of ingredients for all the items required in the individual recipes you are planning to use. If all the ingredients are not on your shelf, check for substitutions. Certain ingredients, such as dried mushrooms, require soaking time. This can be done in the morning—just leave them in water on the kitchen sink or in the refrigerator.

Preparing ingredients should be done in a relaxed atmosphere. And, for some items, don't hesitate to recruit the youngsters' help (i.e., stemming Chinese peas, etc.). I find this preparation time to be an excellent time of the day to listen to my favorite music. Preparing and cooking the ingredients for a Chinese meal can be a great change of pace from your normal routine; it is also an art; it is a part of life.

For example, if a dish calls for onions, celery, bok choy and beef, I would chop or slice these ingredients and place them on a platter with the sliced beef on top. The whole dish can then be moved to the stove when you are ready to cook and the beef, being stir-fried first, will come off the top of the platter first. The vegetables are underneath, ready to be cooked in order.

It is well to have your condiments handy by the stove. Soy sauce, salt, pepper, etc. And have the various dishes you have prepared for cooking arranged on the counter so that those requiring the longest cooking time are closest to the *wok*.

Another practice I have found to be very handy is to program the cooking to prevent confusion and save time. If I am intent on having soup, that goes on the stove first. This allows adequate time for the stock to become aromatic and tasty. The next step is to wash and start the rice on the stove. Now you have more than twenty minutes to leisurely cut and prepare the ingredients for the remainder of the dishes while the soup is simmering and the rice is steaming. When everything is prepared, you can relax until *wok* time. If your work is laid out this way, the food can be cooked just before you and your guests are ready to eat—and it can be served hot.

NOTE: It is also very practical to clean up as you go along—like rinsing the chopping board, washing, drying, and putting away the cleaver, etc. This keeps everything orderly and efficient.

I would like to mention at this point that a *wok* is by far the best utensil in which to cook Chinese and many other recipes because it

Introduction

allows intense even heat to circulate upwards around the *wok* bowl; it is wide enough and deep enough for all the cooking you will need to do; and it is easily cleaned. However, a ten-inch chicken fryer, or skillet, with a tight-fitting cover will do. Rinse out the *wok* after cooking each dish so that there is no intermingling of flavors. Now you can see why cooking, Chinese style, is such fun and offers such mental diversion! Enjoy!

For balance and interest, be bold! Have fun! Discover and become amazed at your own adaptability, versatility and, most of all—your culinary skills!

My fondest hope is that your curiosity, interest and practical application of cooking, Chinese style, will enrich your mode of living and that this book will become a part of your *wok* through life.

chinese foods

Grocery shopping, the time-honored Chinese way, is done quite differently from the manner in which most American housewives buy their family food. Most American homemakers plan their meals ahead, then shop. Chinese cooks plan their meals while they are shopping.

I learned the hows, whys and fun of marketing, Chinese style, as a youngster in San Francisco. I remember well the three blocks from my father's store on Grant Avenue into the heart of Chinatown where we went to shop.

I can still picture the gift and curio shops and, most importantly, the many grocery stores with their myriad wares crowded on open shelves and their fresh produce displayed in bamboo baskets on the sidewalks in front of each store; the poultry shops with their live ducks and chickens cackling away in cages, stacked one on top of the other; the customers, bustling in and out, would select the bird for that night's dinner, then rush off to do other shopping while the poultry-shop owner weighed and priced the whole bird, then killed, feathered and dressed it.

I can clearly recall the fascination I felt at the hundreds of items I saw on the grocery shelves...not knowing what they were or how they were used. I knew they had many colors and shapes and that there was always in intermingling of unusual and exotic aromas.

I remember well the fish markets with the marble-top sink display counters. And the many varieties of fish—fresh rock bass, cod, perch, squid and shrimp—all laid out below the ever-present hanging scales used for quick weighing and pricing. I can still see the dexterous hands that scaled and cleaned the fish, then wrapped them in weeks-old newspapers for carrying home. And, of course, the galvanized tubs, half full of water containing the greatest miracle of all—the live fish and live water snails!

After toddling along on those shopping tours with my father often enough to learn where each store was located, one day—at age five—I was given the responsibility of shopping for the evening meal. The list was written in Chinese, with prices—not weights—noted for each item needed. For example: 15¢ worth of pork or 5¢ worth of *bok choy*, etc. I was given exact change so there could be no mistake. One of the most interesting things about the list was the request for "gimmes"—necessary for seasoning or garnishing the dishes. A little parsley, a few stalks of green onions, a little bit of fermented black beans, a spoonful of bean paste—and my reward, a handful of dried spiced olives that, for some reason, I always finished eating before I was a block away from the grocery store!

In these great days of supermarkets and national food distribution of packaged, fresh and frozen, unprocessed and processed, canned and bottled, precut meats and delicatessen-prepared dinners, the housewife or home chef has very little difficulty obtaining just about any food item she or he might want.

In the case of Chinese ingredients, most supermarkets and specialty stores carry basic seasonings, ingredients or reasonable substitutes for the preparation of Chinese foods. One happy fact about Chinese cookery is that countless varieties of delicious recipes and dishes can be prepared with a very limited number of condiments or ingredients.

The fun and economy of Chinese-style marketing is largely dependent on your not having too many preconceptions when you go to the grocery store. Make your food-buying decisions when you see what is available at a reasonable price.

Many vegetables are seasonal, so take advantage of the laws of supply and demand and purchase them when they are most plentiful and least expensive. Sometimes, even when certain foods are in season, they are high-priced because of a poor harvest. A wise Chinese cook will not be caught up in such circumstances. If bell peppers are high, substitute celery or zucchini. If the cuts of beef are high, get round steak or switch to chicken.

There are several processors of Chinese vegetables, so Chinese vegetables, bean sprouts, water chestnuts and bamboo shoots are most likely readily available. If you want to extend the variety of these canned and frozen items, add fresh carrots, celery, onions, peas, cabbage, etc.

Enjoy your trips to the food market. Be adventurous and economical in your grocery shopping. Stimulate your imagination as to what would also stimulate the palates of your loved ones.

A list of Chinese grocery stores is included in the back of this book. These stores will accept mail orders if you are unable to obtain certain items in your area.

chinese vegetables

Chinese vegetables are neither unique nor exotic. They have graced the tables of Chinese families for many centuries. Now, with the spreading popularity of Chinese food in America, they are no longer considered foreign foods. Chinese vegetables make up a good part of the bulk of the dishes you and your family can enjoy at the thousands of restaurants and take-out kitchens across the country that specialize in Chinese and oriental food. Increasing numbers of these food items are turning up in the canned-food sections and the frozen-food counters of leading supermarkets from coast to coast. From the bean sprouts, water chestnuts and bamboo shoots you can find in cans, to the bok choy (Chinese chard), napa (Chinese cabbage), bean sprouts and ginger roots you find at the fresh produce counters: these vegetables are becoming increasingly popular and commonplace.

Following are the more available Chinese vegetables and suggestions on American substitutes that can be used as alternatives in Chinese dishes.

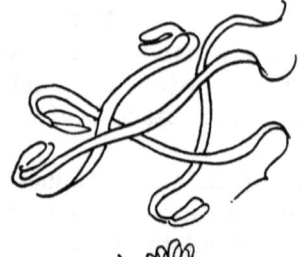

Bean sprouts: Tender, crisp shoots from the mung bean. Most versatile.

Bok choy: Chinese chard, a leafy vegetable about 9 to 12 inches high with white stems and dark green leaves.

Chinese cabbage: Napa. A leafy vegetable with close-packed leaves, white stems and pale green leaves.

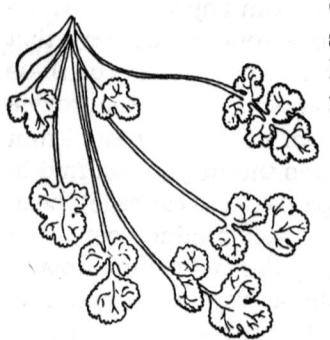

Chinese parsley: Similar to cilantro. Long slender stems and flat palmlike leaves. Has very delicate flavor and is often used as a garnish.

Chinese Foods

Mustard greens: The popular mustard green vegetable used in soups and stir-fried dishes.

Chinese peas: Often referred to as snow peas or peapods. The whole pod is used, except for the stem which is trimmed off before cooking.

Fresh ginger root: A tuber with many offshoots. Has a rich tan or beige scaly skin. A primary seasoning for Chinese cooking. Can also be purchased candied, preserved in syrup or pickled.

Lotus root: A tuberous root of the water lily plant. Can also be purchased in dehydrated form. Light brown in color.

Bitter melon: Dark to light green knobby squash. Bitter to the taste but with a delightfully cooling aftertaste.

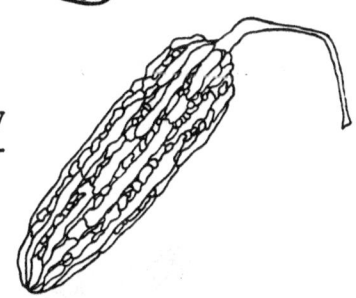

Water chestnuts: More like a bulb than a nut. Dark brown in color. Can be purchased peeled and sliced or whole (canned and frozen).

Bamboo shoots: Young shoots of the bamboo plant. Usually purchased in the can peeled, in chunks or sliced.

Chinese broccoli: Similar in color to the American-grown variety, except the stems are narrower and the leaves are broader.

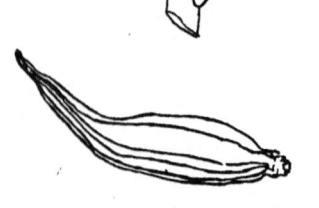

Chinese ochre: A dark green gourd-shaped squash with prominent ridges along its length. Has a sweet flavor. Excellent in soups or stir-fried.

Matrimony vine: A thorny vine with small, dark green leaves. Used as an ingredient and seasoning for soup.

Chinese Foods

Fuzzy melon: Round, elongated squash with a fine fuzzy outer peel. Light to dark green in color. Good cooked many ways.

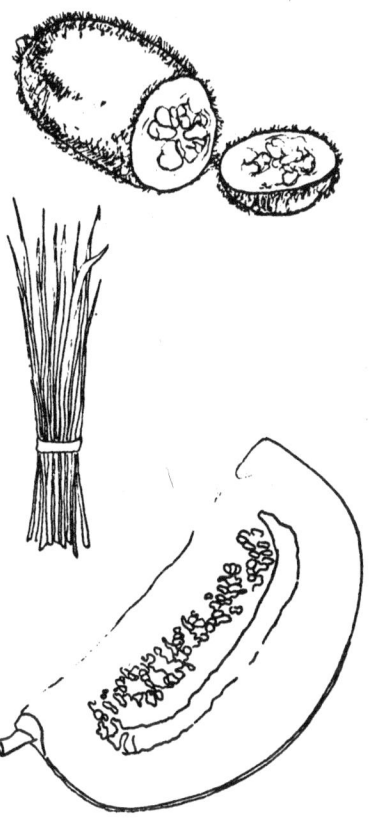

Chinese chives: Like leeks. Narrow, elongated with single leaves. Dark green in color. Good, when used sparingly, instead of scallions. Fantastic stir-fried with ham and eggs!

Winter melon: Watermelon-sized. Wonderful in soups or stir-fried in chunks. Used whole as Winter Melon *Joong*, a gourmet's soup delight.

Chinese long beans: Long string beans about 1/4 inch in diameter and 10 to 18 inches in length. Dark green in color. Crisp and crunchy when cooked.

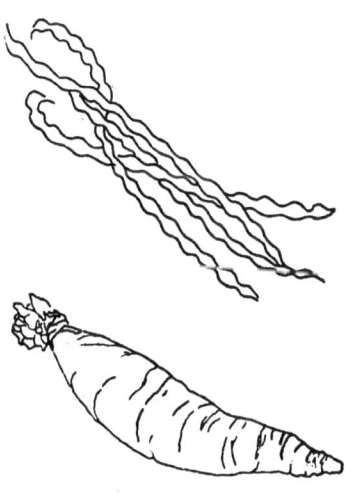

Chinese turnips: Large white root. Excellent as fresh-cooked vegetable. Also makes a good pickle. Is often sold dehydrated or preserved. It has a pungent odor and is used extensively as a seasoning for soups, congee, pork dishes and steamed fish.

american substitutes for chinese vegetables

Since the creation of Chinese food is the result of the method of preparing and cooking the ingredients, other vegetables can often be substituted for Chinese vegetables without perverting the recipe. These substitutes can be used singly or in combination with Chinese vegetables. In making such substitutions, your primary concern should be for the texture of the dish rather than its flavor. The taste of the dish will vary slightly because of natural differences, but the results will be no less enjoyable. Have fun and experiment! Maybe you'll experience the excitement of some new discoveries!

Leafy Green Vegetables

lettuce
cabbage
spinach
chard
turnip tops
beet tops

Bean Sprouts

French-cut string beans
shredded cabbage

Root Vegetables
bamboo shoots, water chestnuts

asparagus
carrots
celery root
rutabagas
parsnips

turnips
Spanish onions
bell peppers
celery
summer squash

Squash and Melon

cauliflower
zucchini
eggplant
broccoli
summer squash

Chinese Parsley

chopped or slivered scallions
chives
shredded lettuce

Chinese Snow Peas

sliced celery
peas
sliced fresh mushrooms

chinese condiments and ingredients

Following is a list of some of the most popularly available ingredients that are called for in various Chinese recipes:

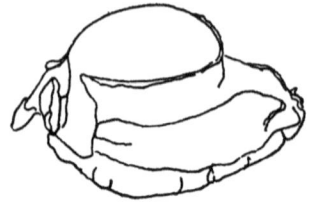

Abalone: A mollusk available in cans or dehydrated. Processed abalone has a brownish color and a resilient texture. Excellent with oyster sauce.

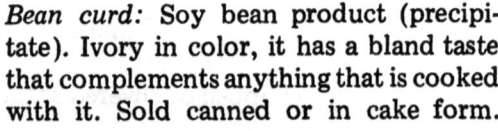

Anise: Eight-pointed, starlike, brown seed with licoricelike flavor and aroma. Used for red-cooked meats.

Bean curd: Soy bean product (precipitate). Ivory in color, it has a bland taste that complements anything that is cooked with it. Sold canned or in cake form.

Fermented bean curd: Small cakes of bean curd fermented in an alcohol solution. Has a tart, pungent flavor. Can be eaten plain or used as a seasoning. Also packed with hot peppers.

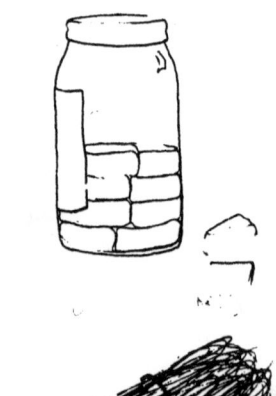

Bean threads: Fine, translucent, brittle noodles made from beans. They have a silky texture and must be soaked in water before using. Can also be deep-fried for a crisp, crackling texture.

Chinese Foods

Birds nest: A gelatinous substance obtained from the nests of the swift. Purified and processed, it is the identifying ingredient of the popular Birds Nest Soup.

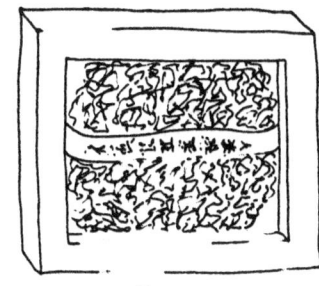

Chinese sausage: A cured, slightly sweet-flavored sausage. Delicious either steamed or as a seasoning meat with vegetables. Also made with liver.

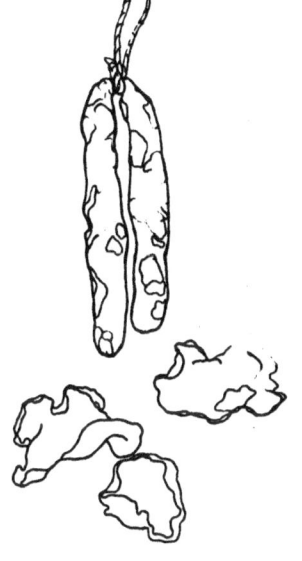

Cloud's ear fungus: A dried cultivated fungus. Grayish in color, when soaked it swells many times into a brownish earlike shape. Has a pleasant, smooth, crunchy texture. A welcome addition to most stir-fried dishes.

Dried Chinese cabbage: Dehydrated Chinese chard. Easily stored and available for a wonderful soup.

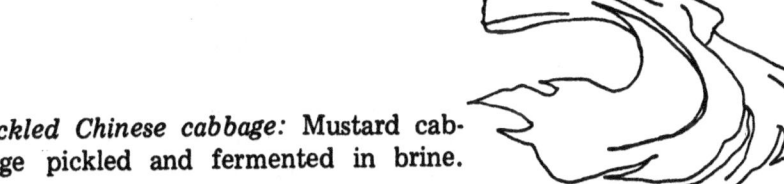

Pickled Chinese cabbage: Mustard cabbage pickled and fermented in brine.

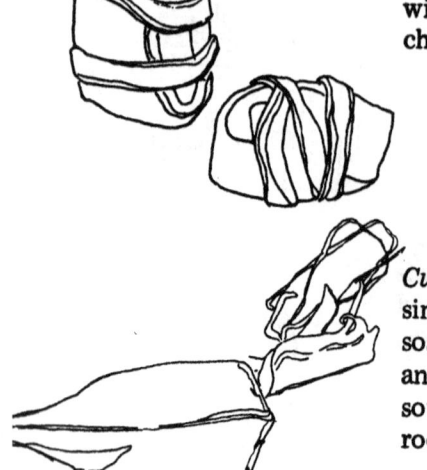

Salt-cured turnips: Two-inch, tightly wrapped, rounded cubes of cured turnips with tops. Must be soaked and finely chopped for use with pork, fish and soups.

Cuttlefish: A dried mollusk, larger but similar to the commercial squid. Must be soaked in water before using. A flavoring and blending agent in slowly cooked soups. It is used most often with lotus root.

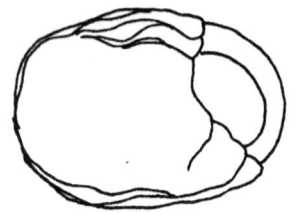

Salted duck eggs: Duck eggs cured in brine about forty days. Packed in black clay. Can be eaten as flavoring additive to meats, or hard-boiled as a separate dish.

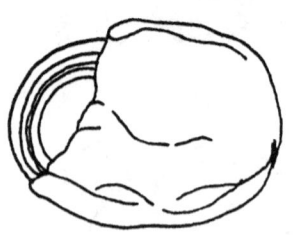

Preserved eggs (1,000 Year Egg): Duck eggs coated with a lime packing and buried for about ninety days. The eggs "set" during this period. The white of the egg acquires a translucent color while the yolk somehow acquires a beautiful character somewhat like concentric circles in deep olive greens. To me, thousand-year eggs are the essence of gastronomic delight. Serve them sliced as an appetizer, accompanied with pickled ginger slices, or steamed with chicken eggs.

Black mushrooms: Dried brownish-black capped mushrooms. Must be soaked in water before using.

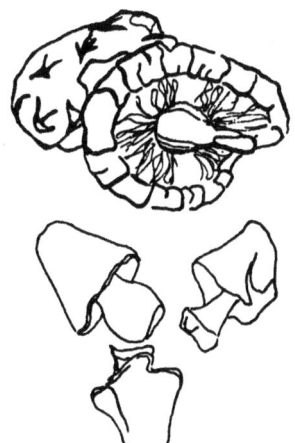

Grass mushrooms: Thin, crisp, leafy, tasty. Best used with steamed chicken.

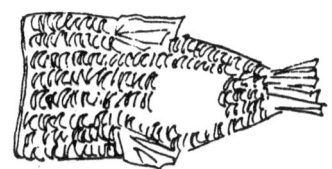

Salted dried fish: Different varieties of fish that are salted and dried. (Some are preserved in oil.) Should be scalded with boiling water before using. Can be deep fried or steamed with pork. Use sparingly.

Dried lily buds (Gold Needles): Dried lily buds, golden yellow in color, about 1/4 inch in diameter and 2 to 4 inches long. Use as a flavoring vegetable with pork, poultry or fish and soups.

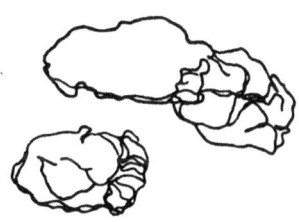

Dried oysters: Sun-dried, flavorful. Should be soaked before using. For flavoring soups and minced meat dishes.

Pickled scallions: Pickled base portion of scallions. Use with preserved eggs and in sweet-and-sour dishes, slivered.

Red dates: Small red dried jujubes used as a flavoring for soups and fish.

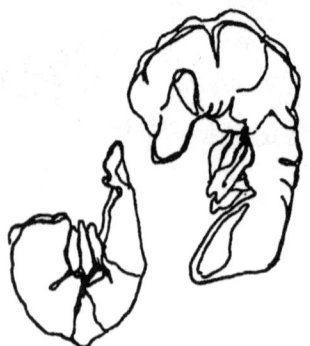

Dried shrimp (large and small): Used as a seasoning for soups and stir-fried vegetable or egg dishes.

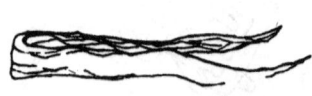

Foo jook (soybean skins): Made from dried soybean milk. Flat, thin, glossy, antique yellow strips. Brittle until soaked Good in soups and stir-fried or simmered dishes.

Salted black beans: Salted and fermented small black beans. Salty and pungent in flavor. Should be soaked in water a little while before mashing to use. Usually used in combination with garlic.

Sweet pickled cucumbers (Tea Melon or Tea Pickles): Dark amber-colored sweet pickle, crunchy and about 3 inches long. Available in cans and jars. Used in congee or steamed pork or beef dishes. Also as a garnish for fish.

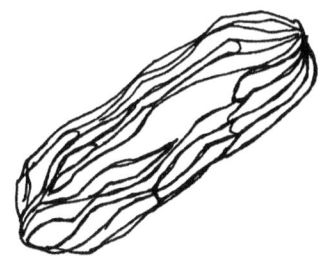

Dried tangerine peel: Dried segments of mandarin oranges that impart a mouth-watering "golden" flavor when used. Use sparingly.

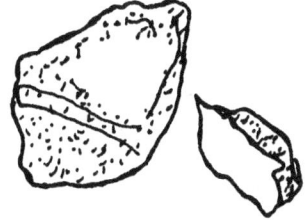

Lotus seeds: One-half inch oval, ivory-colored water lily seeds.

Garlic: A bulbous perennial of the onion family. Used extensively as a seasoning. Can be used crushed or minced. Best purchased in bulb form. Cloves should be firm.

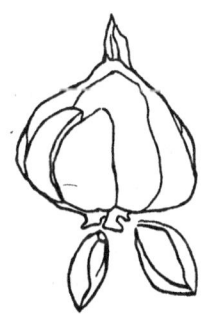

Ingredients Available in Supermarkets

Cornstarch: Powdered corn or corn flour. Used as a thickening agent for gravies and a sealer for meats. Should be blended with cold water before using to prevent lumps in sauces.

Curry powder: Yellow seasoning powder made from ground mustard, fennel, cumin and tamarind spices.

Ham—cured smoked pork: Used as a meat ingredient, a seasoning or a garnish.

Monosodium glutamate: A white crystalline extract of grains and vegetables. Used in China for many centuries. It is said to possess the qualities of enhancing flavor when added sparingly to marinades, sauces and cooked dishes. It is marketed under many trade names including: Ajinomoto, Ve-Tsin, Accent, and MSG.

Mustard: Table condiment often used as a dip. Made by mixing powdered English mustard and water. Hot, pungent.

Oil: Vegetable (corn or peanut) oil. Best for Chinese cooking.

Sesame seeds: Seeds from an East Indian herb. Minute in size, beige in color and possessing the readily identified sesame flavor that is enhanced when the seeds are toasted. Use sparingly as a seasoning and garnish.

Ingredients Available in Chinese Grocery Stores

Dried seaweed: Dark, purplish-colored, thin sheets of dehydrated seaweed. Wonderful for soup.

Egg-roll skins: Egg dough wrappings used for making egg rolls. Can be frozen for future use.

Five-spices: A ready-mixed powder of star anise, fennel, cloves, cinnamon, and anise pepper. Used sparingly in seasoning red-cooked poultry.

Won ton skins: Wrappings used to make won ton by enclosing various minced meats in them. They can be fried, deep-fried, boiled or steamed and may be frozen for future use. They are available in some neighborhood markets in the major metropolitan oriental communities.

sauces for seasoning

Soy sauce: Fermented savory, salty, dark-brown colored sauce made from soybeans, yeast and salt. It is the essential ingredient in Chinese cooking.

Light soy sauce: Made from soybean extracts, flour, salt and sugar. Used as a table condiment and light seasoning.

Dark soy sauce: Made with the same ingredients as light soy sauce with the addition of caramel.

Heavy soy sauce: Made with molasses; thick-bodied. Used to apply color and taste as on spareribs.

Oyster sauce: Made with a concentrate of oysters, soy sauce and brine. Used as a seasoning alone and also to enhance other natural flavors in cooked ingredients.

Sesame oil: Nutlike, fragrant, amber-colored oil made from sesame seeds. Use sparingly—a few drops at a time. Ideal when used in combination with oyster sauce.

Hoy sin sauce: Thick, reddish-brown sauce made from soybeans, garlic and spices. Sold in cans and bottles.

Plum sauce: Thick reddish-brown sauce made with preserved plums. Used as a dip. Especially good with roast duck.

Shrimp paste: Strong, salty shrimp-flavored paste used as seasoning.

Rice wine: Light yellow wine made from rice. Used as a penetrating agent in marinades. If unavailable, substitute dry sherry.

tea

Tea may be called the national beverage of China. Legend has it that Emperor Shen Hung discovered tea in 2737 B.C. and decreed that his subjects drink it for its health-giving properties. Even today, the Chinese here in America consume tea morning, noon and night. For a pause that refreshes, and as a pleasant stimulant to accompany relaxed conversations, nothing surpasses this great drink of the Orient. In China or Chinatown, it is the custom for families and businessmen to *yum cha* (go to drink tea). *Yum cha* is the name for a luncheon or brunch of *dim sum,* a variety of cooked appetizers that are eaten appreciatively with tea.

There are many varieties of tea. Each is native to a particular locale and to specific floral additives which give the tea a special fragrance and delicate flavor. There are two principal tea types: green and red (we know it in the United States as black tea).

Green tea leaves are withered and dried naturally. These leaves are usually the young tender leaves, picked from the top of the shrub. Black tea leaves are produced by various methods of curing; then they are dried, rolled and packed.

Tea shrubs grow about three to five feet tall and are members of the camellia family. The plants have dark green leaves and white blossoms. The Chinese have developed these plants to such a degree of sophistication that they are able to harvest the leaves three times a year, even shrubs growing in poor soil.

A connoisseur of teas is familiar with many varieties and enjoys each one like a connoisseur of wine. For simplicity, I will detail some of the most popularly available teas.

Green Teas

Loong Jeng (Dragon's Well): From Hangchow. Fresh amber color. Delicate flavor and aroma.

Loong Sow (Dragon's Whiskers): From Kwangtung. Light, fresh amber color. Delicate flavor and aroma

Black Teas

Keemun: From Kiangsu and North China. Full-bodied. Rich aroma and bouquet.

Oolong (Black Dragon): From South China and Formosa. Most common tea for family and restaurant use. Slightly pungent and well-flavored.

Jasmine: From Canton and Formosa. Black tea dried with fresh jasmine buds. Pale yellow, delicately aromatic.

Lichee: From Formosa. Black tea dried with yellow lichee blossoms. Pleasantly aromatic with a distinctively light, sweet taste.

Po Nay: From Szechwan. Full-bodied. Deep reddish-amber in color. Wonderfully refreshing with meals. Usually packed in disks about 9-inches in diameter.

To keep it from losing its flavor, tea should be stored in cans or jars with airtight lids. Dry tea leaves, although hardy in appearance and texture. are really quite delicate. They easily absorb other flavors and moisture, losing their own aromatic essence when exposed to the open air too long.

Brewing Tea

Porcelain teapots are best to use for steeping tea. Metallic pots affect the flavor. One-half to one teaspoon of tea is sufficient for each cup of water.

1. First rinse the teapot with hot water. This will help maintain the temperature of the water when it is poured into the pot.

2. Measure the amount of tea leaves and drop them into the pot.

3. Over the leaves in pot, pour boiling water almost to the top. Cover and steep 3 to 5 minutes.

Note: The second steeping of tea is usually better, because the tea leaves have expanded to full size through the absorbtion of water in the first steeping. Just add a pinch more leaves to the pot before adding more boiling water.

Note: The Chinese don't use cream, sugar or lemon in tea because each of these additives deteriorates the natural flavor and aroma of the delicately scented teas.

wines and spirits

China has not added greatly to the world's long list of fine wines and liqueurs. Traditionally, the Chinese, either because of economy or the desire to savor the full body, aroma and pleasing sensations of it, always sip wine. At banquets, wine is sipped between each course to toast the health and good fortune of the host's guests, honored personalities and the host himself.

Chinese wines are not really wines because they are made of grains rather than grapes. They are sipped, used in cooking and included in medicinal brews with herbs. The two main types are white and yellow.

The following short list contains the Chinese wines most commonly available in the U.S.:

Sooching: Common yellow rice wine used primarily for cooking purposes.

Kaoling: White wine distilled from Kaoling, a grain native to North China, similar to vodka.

Ng Gah Pei: Heavy dark orange-yellow wine flavored with herbs. This 96 proof wine is native to Canton and is the favorite liquor served at Chinese banquets. It is very potent and is best enjoyed and appreciated by taking very small sips as you would your favorite brandy or liqueur.

Mui Kwai Lo (rose wine): Clear, 96 proof, with the fragrance of rose petals. Again, a sipping wine.

utensils and food preparation

砂鍋

the wok

The *wok* is almost as ancient and venerable as China itself and most likely is the original portable stove. I have no reason to doubt that *wok* units such as the one pictured above were used by the Chinese immigrants in the holds or on the decks of the ships that brought them from China. I'm sure they were used in the camps that sprang up around the gold fields and the railroads in the middle of the last century.

Simple as it first appears, the *wok* is one of the most versatile cooking utensils ever developed by man. It can be used for every cooking method except roasting or broiling. Having been designed for quick, even heating using a minimum of fuel, it provides maximum cooking surface for small or large quantities of food, is portable and easily cleaned, and is durable, reasonable in cost and fun to use.

Despite all the modern conveniences and cooking utensils the latest technology has put at the housewife's disposal, *woks* are still available and selling better than ever. They can even be purchased in models that are electrically operated. Although several types of *woks* have been designed for home use, I recommend the 13 or 14-inch *wok* as being very practical for most aspects of Chinese cooking.

Types of Woks

(a) Standard *Wok* Unit. Consisting of a lid, a *wok*, and a circular adapter to hold the *wok* firmly in place when in use. Two handles. Use over coals or gas burners.

(b) One-handle *wok*. *Wok* with one wooden handle. A bit easier to handle. Usually 14-inch diameter. Use with lid, adapter, and steam tray.

(c) Flat bottom *wok*. Same as standard *wok* but has flat bottom. Used with lid. Adapter not necessary. Flat bottom makes good contact with heating element on electric stoves possible.

(d) Electric *woks*. American manufactured and designed, Teflon coated. Consists of lid with plastic handle; *wok* with plastic stand and thermostatic heat control.

the cleaver

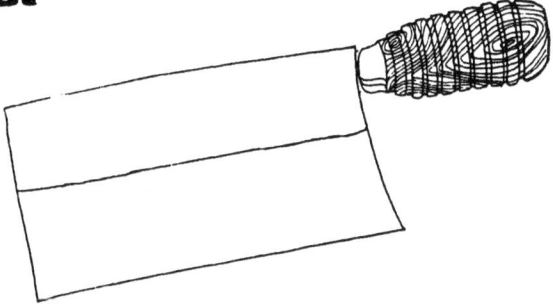

In China, the instrument we Americans know as the cleaver is called *choy doe*—the vegetable knife. It is a versatile household tool with many uses, but is used most often in the kitchen to cut, slice, chop, mince, dice, grind and otherwise prepare foods for the daily meals. For most Chinese, the cleaver is the basic instrument of survival. It might amuse you to know that when I worked as a houseboy, I carried a cleaver around—tucked in my belt. I didn't carry it for protection, but as the all-purpose gardening and yard-work tool to use for trimming, weeding, breaking up the soil and chopping kindling wood!

In combination with a good chopping block or cutting board, the cleaver becomes an important part of the production center for preparing Chinese dishes. It should always be kept very sharp. This makes food preparation much more effortless. The illustrations below describe and explain most of the common kitchen uses for this tool. In addition, you can use the cleaver's handle as a pestle to mash and grind ginger root, garlic and other condiments. You will also find that a very simple hint such as using your cleaver as a spatula will definitely save you lots of tool switching and lots of time. Try sliding the chopped, diced or minced ingredients onto the flat of the blade and transferring these bits and pieces in one swift motion to a bowl, platter or pot. A careful time-and-motion study has proven the labor-saving advantages of this kitchen technique.

Use of the Cleaver

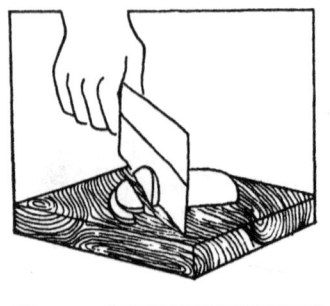

When using the cleaver, the flat of the blade should glide across the knuckles of the fingers holding the material to be cut. The fingers should be curled in such a way that the fingertips are out of the way of the downward stroke of the blade.

In slicing, use a forward cutting motion of the cleaver and guide the blade with the other hand by holding that which is being cut firmly and gradually moving the fingers away as the curring proceeds.

In diagonal cutting, hold item being cut firmly in position so ingredients can be cut on the bias.

In dicing, slice ingredient in 1/4-inch strips, stack evenly, and cut across into 1/4-inch pieces or whatever size is desired.

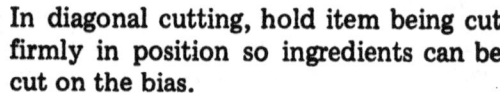

chopsticks

Chopsticks are the very practical and simple instruments used in Chinese cooking and eating. No one knows exactly where or when the name *chopsticks* originated, but the direct translation from the Cantonese, *fii gee* (quick ones), is appropriate to their function since *chop* is pidgin English for *quick*.

Utensils and Food Preparation

Most Chinese chopsticks used for eating are 8 inches to 10 inches long, 1/4 inch in diameter and are slightly tapered, square at one end and round at the other. They are made of wood, bamboo, ivory, silver or plastic. Chinese chopsticks are blunt at the narrow, rounded end in contrast to the Japanese type, which are shaped almost to a point. Disposable chopsticks are also available in individually wrapped envelopes, and must be split apart when needed for use.

Cooking chopsticks come in longer lengths—12 inches to 14 inches. They are very handy for stir-frying, turning ingredients over, picking deep-fried ingredients out of hot oil, stirring soups or vegetables, mixing marinades, beating eggs, sampling and almost any cooking chore you might otherwise do with your fingers.

When eating, chopsticks are used to bring the delectable morsels from the serving dish to the mouth, sometimes with a short pause over the rice in one's bowl. The usual practice today is to furnish serving spoons with each serving dish and individual bowls for rice or soup.

Don't be afraid to try your hand at using chopsticks for preparing and eating Chinese foods. With practice, comes dexterity. Once mastered, they will become indispensable tools.

Use of Chopsticks

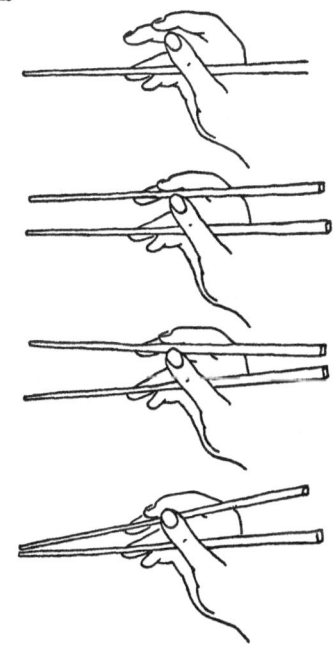

(a) Place one chopstick firmly in cradle between thumb and forefinger, bracing against third finger as shown.

(b) Place second chopstick as shown, and hold as you would a pencil.

(c) Holding the bottom chopstick, move the upper chopstick up and down so that the points meet, as in diagram (d) below.

(d) The points of the chopsticks should be even at all times. To pinch the morsels of food firmly, it is advantageous to hold the chopsticks above the midpoint, for better leverage.

Chinese Kitchen Tools

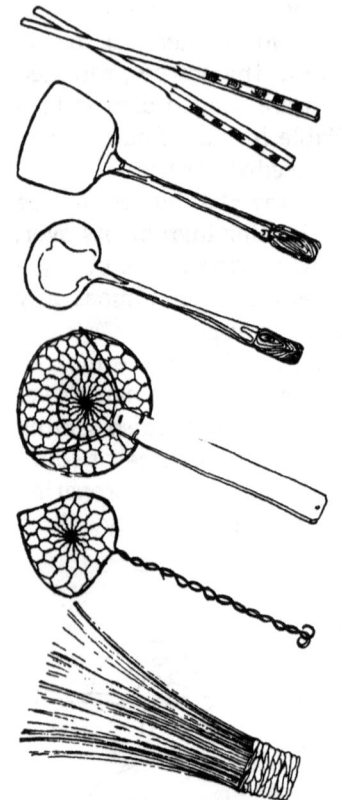

Chopsticks: Wood or bamboo all-purpose tools used in mixing, stirring, packing, tasting.

Spatula: Metal with slightly curved edge to conform to contour of the *wok*.

Scoop: Metal bowl-shaped spoon with handle attached.

Strainer: Wire mesh with split bamboo handle.

Egg Strainer: Wire mesh and handle.

Wok Brush: Bamboo fibers used to clean *wok*.

methods of preparing and cooking chinese food

Chinese cookery involves certain unique methods and techniques of preparing and cooking the ingredients for each dish.

Methods

Stir-frying: The quick or "flash" method of cooking ingredients with a little hot oil in a *wok*, or skillet. This method involves stirring and mixing the ingredients with chopsticks, spatula or wooden spoon until they are cooked as desired.

Braising: Ingredients are stir-fried a few seconds at high heat to mix and coat with oil. Then they are covered and allowed to simmer at a lower heat in their own liquids or in a very little water or soup stock, until done.

Red-Stewing: Ingredients are first braised or fried, then simmered in a liquid or sauce containing a larger portion of soy sauce.

Steaming: Ingredients are steam-cooked in a bowl or on a plate that is raised above the boiling water level by a rack. This process occurs in a covered pot. A practical rack can be devised by punching holes in the bottom of a one-pound coffee can and standing it bottomside up in the water.

Double-Boiling in Steam: The same as steaming, except the ingredients are contained in a deep heat-proof porcelain or metal container with a close-fitting cover. The ingredients may or may not be braised before steaming in their own juices. This is the method my father used frequently to brew a wonderful concoction with beef, select herbs and a little wine. It was a delicious broth possessed of medicinal qualities that strengthen the blood and raised the spirit.

Deep-Frying: The ingredients are completely immersed in hot oil and cooked until golden brown or crisply done. This process requires high heat.

Roasting: Ingredients are cooked in a heated oven for a specific length of time. Generally, the temperature and the timing are determined by the size and type of the items to be roasted.

Barbecuing: Ingredients are cooked in direct heat over pit or open-hearth unit on skewers or hung from racks. (Broiling is a reasonable substitute method.)

Boiling: Ingredients are cooked in actively boiling water or soup stock until done.

Preparation

Soaking: Certain ingredients should be soaked in water well in advance of their cooking time. Vegetables such as spinach, parsley, celery, etc., should be soaked in cold water in the sink or a pan. This restores the vegetables to market freshness. With leafy vegetables such as Chinese cabbage or lettuce, I usually tear off and soak only the amount of leaves I wish to use for a particular meal. With dried ingredients such as Chinese mushrooms, shrimp, etc., I save the water and include it in the measure of liquid used in recipes. Reason—flavor.

Cutting and Slicing: If recipes call for meats that require marinating, always cut or slice the meats first; then, add the marinating ingredients, i.e., garlic or ginger root. This saves time because the meats can be marinating while the vegetables are being prepared.

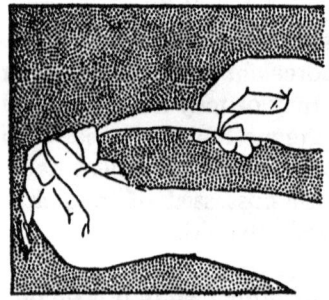

To Devein and Shell Shrimp: Remove heads. Using serrated fruit knife, cut up dorsal side of shrimp 1/4-inch deep.

Open incision, remove shell and wash away vein. If it is desirous to leave tail on, then cut only to base of tail.

Note: It is advantageous to have sufficient bowls and platters on hand for the different dishes you are going to cook. I usually arrange the ingredients on platters or in bowls I choose to serve the dishes in. This saves clean-up and dishwashing time later.

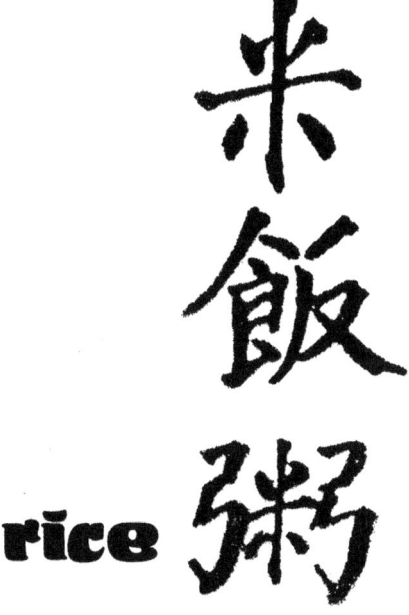

rice

I don't remember exactly how old I was, but I do remember that the very first food I ever cooked was rice; it was imported from China in woven reed sacks, tied with rattan lacing.

Rice was, and still is, the staple food of most Chinese-Americans. But it is no longer just an oriental grocery item. It is readily served in most American homes. We have rice cereal, puffed rice, minute rice and rice puddings. It is even thrown at the bride and groom at American weddings. This tradition baffles me. Why not throw rose petals and save the rice for the honeymooners first home-cooked meal?

At any rate, growing and selling rice has become a gigantic business here in the United States. Production is on such a large scale that many rice fields are sown by plane.

Types of Grain

There are two major types of rice grains: the short (or oval) and the long grain. The short grain is popular, particularly among the Japanese people. This grain has been eaten for centuries in Japan. The grains are larger, have a higher water content when cooked and have a tendency to stick together.

The Chinese prefer the long-grain, or "Texas Patna" type of rice. The grains are longer and, when cooked, they become fluffy and loose. My father told me that this difference in preference over the two types of rice accounts for the difference in the size of Japanese and Chinese chopsticks. The pointed, Japanese sticks, have no trouble picking up the clumps of short-grain rice, but the longer Chinese sticks are more suitable for handling the loose, long-grain rice.

how to cook rice

Many people will tell you never to take the lid off the rice pot after it's placed on the stove and starts cooking, otherwise, you will have "bad rice." Their advice may be true if you cook your rice according to the directions in most cookbooks. But, if you follow the directions below for washing and cooking your rice, you won't have any problem. I cover the rice pot when it starts the steaming procedure.

Measurements: 1/2 cup uncooked rice for each person unless a specific recipe calls for more or less.

Washing: At the sink, place the rice in a deep saucepan that has a tight-fitting lid. (Usually the pan in which you will cook the rice.)

Add enough water to cover the rice. Stir a few times with your fingers, using a circular motion. Then carefully pour off the water, allowing the grains to sink to the bottom of the pot.

Scrubbing: Now, all the grains are wet and ready for "scrubbing." While firmly holding the pot with one hand, immerse the slightly cupped fingers of your other hand into the rice. With a rapid circular motion, either clockwise or counterclockwise, stir the grains of rice so that they rub against each other and the pot. (This rubs the starch covering off each grain.)

Rice

Rinsing: Fill the pot 3/4 full of water and stir the rice a few times with the fingers. You will notice that the water will acquire a milky white appearance. This is the starchy substance on the grains that should be carefully poured off with the water.

Repeat the scrubbing and rinsing process 3 or 4 times until the water is clear. Pour off cleansing water.

Cooking: Put enough water in the pot to cover the rice about 3/4 of an inch.

Turn the heating unit on the stove to High and bring water to a boil. Allow boiling to continue until the water boils down to the top level of the rice. (At this point it will be bubbling.)

Immediately place lid snugly on the pot and turn the heat down as low as possible. Keep pot covered over low heat for 20 minutes. During this time, the rice is cooking in its own steam. Now, uncover and stir with chopsticks to make sure it's loose and fluffy and ready to serve.

This may seem a lengthy operation for preparing rice. But, like many recipes, it appears more complicated written out than it actually is. Once you've done it a couple of times, you'll find it very simple, quick and satisfying. Most of all, it will prevent you from producing "bad rice."

Crackling Rice

Generally, a crusty layer of rice will form on the bottom of the pan if the rice remains in it very long after cooking. Some call this *crackling rice* because it is so crunchy when eaten. It is delicious with tea or soup, or even with boiling water. My favorite trick is to add boiling water to the crust and mix in a tablespoon or two of fermented bean cake. It's delicious! Should it be desirable to reheat the rice, simply add a tablespoon or two of water and resteam it, covered, at a low heat.

Extra Rice

You can anticipate a wonderful bowl of fried rice by cooking more rice than would be required for a specific meal. Day-old rice makes the best fried rice because much of the water has evaporated and the grains will remain loose when stir-fried.

Fried rice can be a complete and nourishing meal in itself. It is not only economical, it's easily the most versatile and imaginative of Chinese dishes. It's a wonderful way to utilize those little pieces or portions of meat not quite enough for a serving and too precious to gulp down in a sandwich. The small amount of meat used in fried rice adds mostly flavor and texture. Leftovers are ideal for fried rice dishes, but raw meats can also be used. Raw meats must be stir-fried before being added to the rice.

Note: Should you wish to reheat the rice, simply add a tablespoon or two of water and steam again in the covered pot, at low heat, for a few minutes.

BASIC FRIED RICE
(Plain Fried Rice)
(Serves 4)

3 cups cooked rice
2 eggs, beaten
1 teaspoon salt
2 tablespoons soy sauce
1/4 teaspoon pepper
1 tablespoon peanut oil
3 scallions, chopped

In *wok*, or skillet, heat oil. Add scallions and stir-fry a few seconds. Add rice and balance of ingredients except eggs. Stir-fry until thoroughly mixed. Separate rice in center of *wok* to form opening to bottom. Pour eggs into opening and stir-fry. Mix into rice when they begin to set. Serve immediately.

Rice

Variations

Many variations of the fried-rice recipe above can be made by adding 1/2 cup of any of the following meats, diced. Raw meats should be stir-fried with the scallions.

    Barbecued pork
    Roast pork
    Chicken livers
    Roast chicken
    Chinese sausage
    Salami
    Bologna
    Knackwurst
    Bacon*
    Boiled chicken
    Ham
    Chicken giblets
    Lamb chops
    Roast beef
    Oysters
    Canadian bacon
    Wieners
    Lobster
    Lamb roast
    Boiled chicken
    Roast turkey
    Boiled tongue
    Shrimp
    Dried shrimp (soaked and drained)
    Smoked oysters
    Crab meat
    Kielbasa (Polish sausage)

*Cut 6 slices of bacon crosswise into 1/4-inch pieces. Stir-fry bacon bits until almost done. Add scallions and follow basic recipe, but using bacon grease instead of oil.

rice congee

When I was a boy scout and a member of Troop 3 in San Francisco's Chinatown, one great pleasure enjoyed by us was to walk the street *(hong guy)* after the scout meetings. The route was up one side and down the other of the eight main blocks of Chinatown's Grant Avenue. These walks of fellowship and camaraderie always terminated at a small restaurant, Sam Wo, on Washington Street just off Grant Avenue where we delighted in our favorite evening snack, a bowl of *jook*, or rice gruel, better known as congee. It was garnished with our favorite choice of meats and condiments.

Congee is a thick rice soup made by simmering a small portion of rice several hours in a large quantity of water. After long cooking, the rice breaks down and forms a creamy, bland soup with a distinct texture created by the rice. Congee is very nourishing and easy to eat. It has the versatility of fried rice inasmuch as different combinations of ingredients can make *jook* into a wonderful variety of taste experiences. And, like fried rice, *jook* requires little amounts of ingredients in each bowl because they are included primarily for texture and flavor. It is eaten morning, noon and night and is served piping hot.

Raw ingredients can be cooked in the hot, simmering congee before it is dished up. Cooking time will depend on the type of meat used. Dried scallops, shrimps, or oysters, can be added to the pot when the *jook* is first put on the stove. Raw pork, chicken giblets or beef can be simmered in the *jook* fifteen or twenty minutes. Sliced fish fillets, chopped shrimp, cooked meats, need only a few minutes. A use for the carcass of roast chicken or turkey is a big pot of *jook*. The meat will fall off the bone and the flavor imparted will be a tantalizing surprise.

Congee can be garnished with chopped pickled tea melons, salted turnips, scallions or parsley and chopped nuts. It can be seasoned with soy sauce or oyster sauce with a few drops of sesame oil. Just before serving, a raw egg can be stirred in and cooked to give it a different flavor, texture and body. If kept in the refrigerator, congee will last several days. During this period, it might dehydrate a bit and become thicker. It can be thinned out very easily if so desired by adding a little water.

egg rolls and won ton

egg rolls

This is not a term descriptive of a game played by children on the lawns of parks and exclusive estates at Eastertime, but it *is* a term indicative of spring.

After the celebration of the Chinese New Year, *churn ginn* (spring rolls) were traditionally served with hot tea to visiting relatives and friends. Somewhere along the line, the term *egg rolls* was coined to identify this wonderful delicacy because the wrapping is usually made with a light egg batter.

The wrapping is made first, allowed to cool; then a spoonful or two of specially prepared and cooked ingredients is placed on each "skin" or "pancake," rolled and sealed. The egg rolls are then steamed or deep fried before serving.

There are several ways to make egg roll skins. I prefer the following because it is easier than most recipes and the skins can be made leisurely.

EGG ROLL SKINS
(12)

1-1/2 cups flour
1/4 cup cornstarch
1/2 teaspoon salt
2 eggs, beaten
1-1/2 cups cold water
Peanut oil

Combine flour, cornstarch and salt in a bowl. Blend in the eggs. Slowly add water, stirring in one direction until thin smooth batter is formed. Heat 6-inch skillet over low flame and brush lightly and evenly with oil. Pour 2 tablespoons of batter into pan. Roll and tilt the pan to distribute the batter thinly and evenly in bottom of pan. If bubble holes appear, brush over the batter to seal. Just before skin is brown (as it begins to separate from the sides) remove, place on platter and cover with damp cloth. Repeat until batter is used up.

EGG ROLL FILLINGS

1/4 lb. shredded chicken breast
1/2 teaspoon salt
1/2 teaspoon sugar
1 tablespoon rice wine *or* sherry
1 teaspoon soy sauce
2 tablespoons oil
4 Chinese mushrooms, presoaked and sliced
2 cups blanched bean sprouts
2 scallion stalks, finely slivered into 2-inch lengths
1 tablespoon soy sauce

In bowl, combine chicken, salt, sugar, wine, 1 teaspoon soy sauce, and marinate 20 minutes. Heat oil in *wok*, or skillet, and add chicken. Stir-fry until no longer pink. Add remaining ingredients and stir-fry 2 minutes. Remove to colander to drain and cool.

Egg Rolls and Won Ton

Variations in the ingredients can be made by substituting different shredded meats, i.e., ham, turkey, pork, crabmeat.

Making Egg Rolls

1. Place a portion of filling on wrapper as shown. Fold bottom corner up.

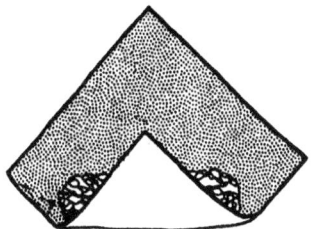

2. Fold over left corner.

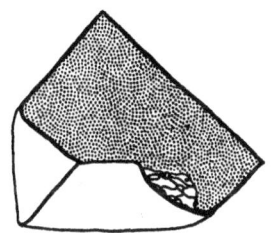

3. Fold over right corner.

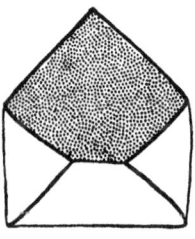

4. Roll into egg-roll shape. Seal loose flap with batter or with beaten egg.

Cooking Egg Rolls

DEEP FRIED

Deep fry in oil 375° until brown. Drain on paper towel. Can be kept hot in warming oven. Egg rolls can be dipped in beaten egg, then in cornstarch before frying, for crunchier skin.

STEAMED

To steam, place on lightly oiled heat-proof platter with separation between rolls to prevent sticking together. Steam 15 to 30 minutes. Less time if filling is precooked.

PANFRIED

In *wok*, or skillet, heat 2 tablespoons oil. Brown egg rolls on all sides. This method is best for rolls with precooked ingredients.

Serving

Egg rolls can be served whole, halved or quartered with a catsup-mustard dip, plum sauce or soy sauce-mustard dip.

won ton

"Meat-filled ravioli . . . like dumplings." That's as close as I can come to a description of won ton or the literal translation, *Swallows of Clouds*.

These specialities are well worth the fun in making, and children at an early age can learn to fill and fold them as their contribution to togetherness.

Won ton wrappings can be purchased in Chinese markets. Many markets carry them in the refrigerator sections. Another source is your favorite Chinese restaurant. But, it is very simple to do it yourself.

Won ton can be deep fried, boiled or steamed.

Egg Rolls and Won Ton 51

Making Won Ton

1. Place portion of filling in center of wrapper.

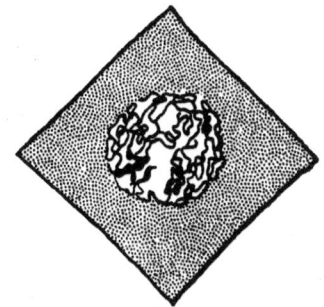

2. Fold lower corner forward as shown.

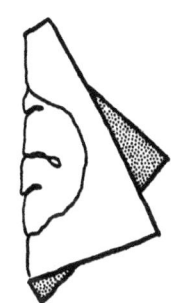

3. Bring outer corners together.

4. Seal with a bit of beaten egg. Pinch together to hold.

BASIC WON TON WRAPPINGS

2 cups flour
1 cup cornstarch
1 teaspoon salt
3 eggs, beaten
2 tablespoons cold water

Sift flour, cornstarch and salt into large mixing bowl. Add eggs and water. Knead into stiff dough. Cover with damp cloth and refrigerate 1 hour. Divide into 2 portions and place on well-floured board. Roll into paper-thin sheets with rolling pin. Dust with flour. Cut into 3-inch strips. Stack, then cut crosswise into 3-inch squares.

WON TON FILLING

1/4 lb. uncooked shrimp, minced
1/4 lb. pork, minced
3 Chinese mushrooms, presoaked and finely chopped
2 tablespoons soy sauce
1/2 teaspoon salt
1/4 teaspoon MSG

Egg Rolls and Won Ton

Combine all ingredients in mixing bowl and mix well.

Note: After filling is used up, the leftover wrappings can be wrapped and refrigerated for later use, or frozen for future use.

FRIED WON TON—PLAIN
(Serves 4)

Deep fry 24 won ton in deep oil until golden brown. Drain on paper towel. Serve with mustard-catsup dip or plum sauce.

FRIED WON TON—SWEET-AND-SOUR
(Serves 4)

1/2 cup diced barbecued pork
1/2 cup pineapple pieces
1/2 cup bell peppers, 1-inch sections
1/4 cup white vinegar
1/4 cup brown sugar
1/4 cup pineapple juice
1 teaspoon catsup
1 teaspoon soy sauce
1 teaspoon oil
1/2 onion, 1-inch squares
1 medium fresh tomato, cut into eights
1 tablespoon cornstarch
1 tablespoon water

Combine vinegar, sugar, pineapple juice, catsup and soy sauce. Set aside. In *wok*, or skillet, heat oil. Add barbecued pork and stir-fry to heat. Add bell peppers, onion, tomato and stir-fry until onion is translucent. Add cornstarch and water mixture, and stir until sauce thickens. Pour over fried won ton.

Note: Ingredients and sauce for topping can easily be varied.

WON TON IN SOUP
(Serves 4)

24 won ton, cooked until soft, drained
4 cups soup stock
1/2 cup chopped, cooked meat
1 scallion, chopped
1/4 cup chopped water chestnuts
1 teaspoon soy sauce
1/2 teaspoon salt
1/4 teaspoon MSG

Combine all ingredients, except won ton, in saucepan. Bring to boil, simmer 3 minutes. Divide cooked won ton into bowls. Fill each bowl with soup.

Note: Any clear soup and combination of ingredients can be used for variety.

appetizers

The French call them hors d'oeuvres. We Americans call them appetizers. But the Chinese call them *dim sum*—that which touches the heart. This last appellation seems the most appropriate to me. Although they can be served as part of the meal, Chinese appetizers are more delightful when served with tea or cocktails during that part of the evening after everything is prepared for cooking and the family or guests have a wonderful chance to chat, visit and exchange expressions of the heart.

I might suggest, not only from the standpoint of simplicity, but also from the practical aspect—that one, two or three items be prepared—depending on the size of the group dining—and that these be kept ready in a warming oven. It is very possible for your guests to fill up on appetizers and minimize their appetite for dinner, so, don't overdo it. Be prepared without overloading the appetizer trays. You can always save those prepared, but not eaten, for the next day.

PORK BALLS
(Serves 4)

3/4 lb. lean pork
2 water chestnuts, peeled
2 Chinese mushrooms, presoaked 2 hours and drained
1 1/4-inch slice fresh ginger root
1 tablespoon water
1-1/2 tablespoons cornstarch
1/4 teaspoon salt
2 teaspoons soy sauce
1/4 teaspoon MSG
Oil for deep frying

On chopping board, with cleaver, mince together pork, water chestnuts, mushrooms and ginger root. In a bowl, mix water and cornstarch into paste. Combine with salt, soy sauce, and MSG. Blend with pork mixture and roll into balls 1-inch in diameter. In *wok*, or skillet, heat oil to 375° and carefully drop pork balls one at a time into oil. Deep fry until dark golden brown. Drain on paper towel. Skewer with cocktail picks. Serve on bed of lettuce with hot mustard and catsup mixture or *hoy sin* sauce.

SHRIMP BALLS
(Serves 4)

3/4 lb. shrimp, shelled and deveined
4 water chestnuts
1 tablespoon minced green onions
1 1/4-inch slice fresh ginger root
2 teaspoons soy sauce
2 tablespoons rice wine *or* sherry
1 egg, beaten
1 tablespoon cornstarch
1/4 teaspoon salt
1/4 teaspoon MSG
Oil for deep frying
Lemon wedges
Shredded lettuce

Mince together shrimp, water chestnuts, green onion and ginger root. In bowl, combine soy sauce, wine, egg, cornstarch, salt and MSG. Add shrimp mixture and blend well. Take one heaping teaspoon of mixture at a time and roll into a ball. In *wok*, or skillet, heat oil to 375°. Place shrimp balls into oil one at a time. Keep turning until they are evenly browned and floating on top of the oil. Drain on paper towel. Skewer with cocktail picks. Serve on bed of finely shredded lettuce with hot mustard and catsup mixture or *hoy sin* sauce.

BEEF BALLS
(Serves 4)

1 lb. lean ground beef
1 egg, beaten
1-1/2 tablespoons cornstarch
1 teaspoon rice wine *or* sherry
2 tablespoons soy sauce
1 teaspoon salt
2 tablespoons oil
1/2 cup water
1/2 teaspoon MSG

Combine lightly beaten egg with 1 tablespoon soy sauce, 1/4 teaspoon salt and 1/4 teaspoon MSG. Combine with cornstarch and wine. Fold in ground beef. Roll meat mixture into 1-inch-diameter balls. Heat oil in *wok*, or skillet, and completely brown beef balls. Add water and remaining soy sauce, salt and MSG. Bring liquid to an active simmer. Cover and cook 30 minutes at low heat.

MARINATED BEEF CHUNKS
(Serves 4)

1-1/2 lb. sirloin *or* flank steak
1/3 cup soy sauce
2 tablespoons sugar
1 1/4-inch slice ginger root, mashed
3 tablespoons rice wine *or* sherry

Place beef in deep bowl or pan. Combine remaining ingredients and marinate beef for 30 minutes. Broil steak 5 minutes on each side, or as desired. Cut into bite-size chunks and serve with cocktail picks.

STEAMED CHINESE PORK SAUSAGE
(Serves 4)

4-6 Chinese pork sausages, rinsed in water

Place sausages on plate, then onto rack in pot with about 1-inch water in bottom. Bring water to boil. Reduce heat. Cover and steam 15 minutes. Remove sausages and slice diagonally into pieces about 1/4-inch thick. Serve with cocktail picks.

Note: If rice is being cooked at this time, after water evaporates sausages may be steamed on top of the rice without a plate. The oil from sausages can then seep into the rice, giving it a very delicate flavor and aroma.

RUMAKI
(Serves 4)

6 chicken livers
9 water chestnuts, peeled and halved
9 slices raw bacon, halved crosswise
1/2 cup soy sauce
1/4 cup water
1 1/4-inch slice ginger root
1 tablespoon rice wine *or* sherry
1/2 teaspoon sugar
1/4 teaspoon MSG
Cocktail picks
Mustard and catsup sauce
Shredded lettuce—*optional*

In saucepan combine soy sauce, water, ginger root, wine, sugar and MSG with chicken livers. Bring to boil and simmer 3 minutes. Remove chicken livers. Drain, then slice each into three pieces. Save liquid. Take one piece of chicken liver, one-half water chestnut and wrap firmly with raw bacon slice. Skewer firmly with cocktail pick. Marinate skewered chicken livers in leftover liquid from first combination of ingredients. Arrange *rumaki* on rack in shallow pan. Heat oven to 400° and roast 10 minutes or until bacon is crisp and brown. Serve on bed of lettuce with mustard and catsup sauce or *hoy sin* sauce.

BACON-WRAPPED WATER CHESTNUTS
(Serves 4)

9 slices lean raw bacon
18 whole water chestnuts, peeled, rinsed and drained
1/3 cup soy sauce
1/4 cup water
1 tablespoon rice wine *or* sherry
1 1/4-inch slice ginger root, finely minced
1/4 teaspoon MSG
1 teaspoon sugar

Cut bacon slices in half crosswise. Firmly wrap each bacon around individual water chestnuts and skewer securely with cocktail pick. In bowl, combine remaining ingredients and marinate bacon-wrapped water chestnuts for 30 minutes. Arrange on rack in shallow pan. Heat oven to 400° and roast 10 minutes or until bacon is done to desired crispness.

STUFFED MUSHROOMS
(Serves 4)

18 medium-sized fresh mushrooms
1/4 lb. lean pork
4 full sprigs Chinese parsley *or* 1 stalk scallion
1 1/4-inch slice ginger root
1 teaspoon soy sauce
1 tablespoon rice wine *or* sherry
1 teaspoon cornstarch
1/4 teaspoon salt
1/4 teaspoon MSG
Additional cornstarch

Wash and peel mushrooms. Remove stems. Mince together mushrooms stems, pork, parsley, ginger root and place in a bowl. Add the soy sauce, wine, cornstarch, salt and MSG, and blend. Divide mixture into 18 portions and roll each into a ball. Place dash of cornstarch into hollow of each mushroom, then firmly press in pork balls. Place stuffed mushrooms on plate and put on rack in *wok* or large pot. Steam covered 30 minutes.

BARBECUE PORK
(Serves 4)

2 lbs. boneless pork butt
4 tablespoon soy sauce
1 tablespoon sugar
1 tablespoon *hoy sin* sauce—*optional*
2 tablespoons honey
1 tablespoon rice wine *or* sherry
2 cloves garlic, mashed
1/4 teaspoon MSG

Cut pork into strips 6x3/4x2 inches. Combine remaining ingredients with pork strips and marinate 2 to 3 hours. Heat oven to 400°. Lay pork strips on rack in shallow pan (or hang with skewers from oven rack with drip pan at bottom. Roast 10 minutes. Reduce heat to 250°. Roast 25 minutes longer or until done. Cut pork strips diagonally across grain into bite-size pieces 1/4-inch thick. Serve with hot mustard and catsup sauce or hot mustard and soy sauce.

THOUSAND-YEAR-OLD EGGS
(Serves 4)

4-6 preserved eggs
Pickled ginger slices, for garnish
Pickled scallions, for garnish

Remove clay and wash eggs well under cold running water. Carefully remove shells and slice eggs with egg slicer or cheese cutter, or quarter lengthwise. Arrange egg slices on plate with ginger and scallions.

Appetizers

BAR-B-CUED SPARERIBS
(Serves 4)

1 slab (4-5 lbs.) pork ribs—*optionally* cut into 2-inch widths by butcher
1 clove garlic, mashed
1 tablespoon brown sugar
4 tablespoons *hoy sin* sauce
1 tablespoon brown bean sauce
2 teaspoons rice wine *or* sherry

Place ribs in shallow pan. Combine remaining ingredients and use to cover ribs. Let stand 2 to 3 hours. Drain. Save marinade. Heat oven to 350°. Place ribs in shallow baking pan, curved side up and roast for 30 minutes. Turn ribs over, baste with marinade and roast another 30 minutes. Turn ribs over, baste and roast last 30 minutes.

BEEF JERKY
(Serves 4)

1 large flank steak (approx. 2-1/2 lbs.)
1/3 cup soy sauce
1 tablespoon Worchestershire sauce
1 clove garlic, peeled and crushed
1/4 teaspoon ginger powder
3 tablespoons rice wine *or* sherry
1/4 teaspoon MSG
1/2 teaspoon liquid smoke—*optional*

Trim off fat from flank steak. Slice lengthwise into very thin strips. Combine remaining ingredients in shallow dish. Marinate meat in mixture, covered, overnight in refrigerator. Arrange meat strips (not overlapping) on baking racks in shallow pans and bake very slowly at 150° for 12 hours. Meat strips may be hung from oven rack on skewers with drip pan at base.

SCALLOPS IN WINE SAUCE
(Serves 4)

3/4 lb. bay scallops
1/4 cup rice wine *or* sherry
3/4 cup soy sauce
2 tablespoons sugar
1 1/4-inch slice ginger root, mashed
1/4 teaspoon MSG

Use whole bay scallops. If sea scallops are used, cut into quarters. In saucepan, combine all ingredients except scallops and bring to a boil. Add scallops and reduce heat. Simmer until liquid is almost gone. Skewer on cocktail picks.

BROILED CHICKEN WITH GIBLETS
(Serves 4)

3 whole chicken gizzards
1/2 lb. chicken livers
2 chicken breasts, boned
1/2 cup soy sauce
1/4 cup rice wine *or* sherry
2 tablespoons sugar
1 1/4-inch slice ginger root, mashed
1/4 teaspoon MSG
Lettuce leaves

Wash gizzards and cut lengthwise individually into 4 pieces. Cover with water in saucepan and cook for 10 minutes. Drain. Cut chicken meat and livers into 12 pieces. Skewer gizzards, chicken and liver pieces alternately on cocktail picks and arrange on oiled broiling pan. (Bottom of pan can be lined with foil for easy clean up.) Combine soy sauce, wine, sugar, ginger and MSG in small saucepan. Bring to boil, then brush liquid over skewered meats. Broil the meat 12 minutes, turning and basting with liquid several times. Place on bed of lettuce and serve.

Appetizers

MEATBALLS IN MUSHROOM SAUCE
(Serves 4)

1/2 lb. ground beef
1/2 lb. ground pork
4 water chestnuts, peeled and minced
3/4 teaspoon salt
1/4 teaspoon MSG
1-1/2 tablespoon soy sauce
3/4 cup cornstarch
3 tablespoons oil
1 clove garlic, minced
1/2 teaspoon ginger powder
1/4 cup fresh mushrooms, sliced
1 cup beef broth
2 green onions

In bowl, thoroughly mix beef, pork, water chestnuts, 1/2 teaspoon salt, MSG, soy sauce and 1 tablespoon cornstarch. Shape into balls about 1-inch in diameter. Then roll balls in remaining cornstarch until evenly coated. In *wok*, or skillet, heat oil and brown total surface of meat balls. Add garlic, ginger powder, mushrooms and remaining salt and cook 30 seconds. Add broth and bring to low simmer. Cook for 30 minutes. Serve, garnishing with green onions.

MARINATED MUSHROOM CAPS
(Serves 4)

24 medium fresh mushroom caps
1/4 cup rice wine *or* sherry
4 tablespoons vinegar
2 tablespoons sugar
1/2 teaspoon salt
2 tablespoons soy sauce
2 scallions, chopped

Wash and peel mushroom caps. In saucepan, combine all ingredients. Bring liquid to boiling point. Remove saucepan from stove and let cool. Keep mixture overnight in refrigerator. Drain when ready to serve. Skewer mushroom caps with cocktail picks.

OYSTER FRITTERS
(Serves 4 to 6)

3/4 cup chopped oysters
3 eggs, separated
2 tablespoons sifted flour
1 green onion, finely minced
1 tablespoon finely chopped almonds
1/4 teaspoon salt
1/8 teaspoon white pepper
1 teaspoon soy sauce
1/8 teaspoon powdered ginger
Oil for deep frying
Hot mustard
Catsup

Beat egg yolks and blend with flour, green onion, almonds, salt, pepper, soy sauce and ginger. Beat egg whites until fluffy and fold into egg yolk mixture together with oysters. In *wok*, or skillet, heat oil to 370° and carefully drop one teaspoon oyster batter into oil. Fry, turning occasionally, until completely browned. Drain oyster fritters on paper towel.

ROLLED BEEF BITS
(Serves 4)

1 medium flank steak (approx. 2 lbs.)
Green onions
1/3 cup soy sauce
2 teaspoons sugar
3 tablespoons rice wine *or* sherry
1/4 teaspoon MSG

Cut flank steak into thin 2-inch strips across the grain and curl into small rolls. Wrap green part of onion around meat roll and fasten with cocktail picks. Combine remaining ingredients and marinate meat rolls. Broil about 10 minutes, turning once.

Appetizers

ABALONE WITH PICKLED SCALLIONS
(Serves 4)

1-lb. can whole abalone, cut into 1/8-inch thick slices
Pickled scallions, halved lengthwise—enough pieces to match abalone
Lemon wedges

Wrap abalone slices around scallion quarters and fasten with cocktail picks. Serve with lemon wedges.

PORK AND CRAB MEAT BALLS
(Serves 4 to 6)

1/2 lb. fresh pork butt, minced
2 tablespoons finely chopped mushrooms, canned or fresh
1/4 cup water chestnuts, finely chopped
1/4 teaspoon sugar
Salt *to taste*
White pepper *to taste*
1 teaspoon soy sauce
1/2 cup crab meat
3/4 cup corn flour
1 tablespoon water
1 egg, beaten
Oil to deep fry

In mixing bowl, combine mushrooms, water chestnuts, pork, sugar, salt, pepper and soy sauce. Fold in crab meat. Roll mixture into balls about 1 inch in diameter. Coat pork-and-crab balls in corn flour. Add water to egg and beat. Then dip balls in egg mixture. Deep fry for 5 minutes or until brown. Drain on paper towel and serve with cocktail picks.

SPICY CHICKEN LIVERS
(Serves 4)

1 lb. chicken livers
Water
1/2 cup soy sauce
1/2 cup chopped green onions
1/4 cup rice wine *or* sherry
1 tablespoon sugar
1/4 teaspoon anise seed
2 teaspoons fresh ginger root, minced

Cover livers with water and bring to a boil. Drain well. In saucepan, combine soy sauce, green onions, wine, sugar, anise seed and ginger with livers. Bring to a boil, then cover and simmer 15 minutes. Chill thoroughly. Slice livers into bite-size pieces, return to stock and keep cold. Drain and serve at room temperature.

EGGS STUFFED WITH CRAB
(Serves 4)

1/4 lb. crab meat, fresh or canned
6 hard-cooked eggs, cut into halves
1 tablespoon green onion, finely chopped
1 teaspoon lemon juice
1/4 teaspoon salt
1 teaspoon soy sauce
Dash Tabasco sauce
Mayonnaise
1/8 teaspoon MSG

Chop egg yolks and mix with rest of ingredients, adding enough mayonnaise to moisten the mixture. Refill egg-white halves with crab mixture and serve chilled.

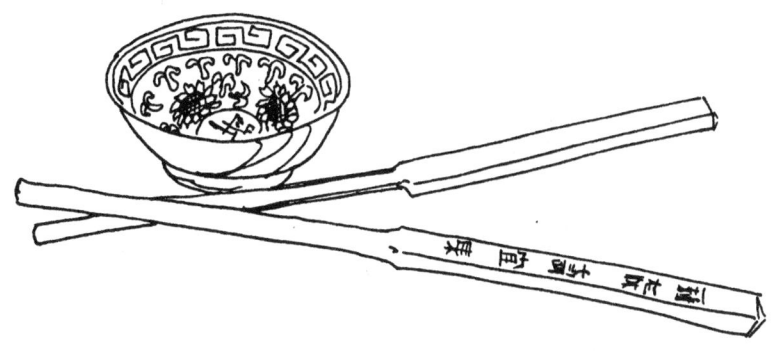

SHRIMP DELIGHT
(Serves 4)

1 lb. raw shrimp, shelled and deveined—approx. 16-20
2 stalks green onions, finely chopped
1 clove garlic, minced
1/8 teaspoon MSG
Peanut oil

Wash shrimp and drain on towel. Pour enough oil to cover bottom of *wok*, or skillet, and sauté or stir-fry shrimp with onions, garlic, and MSG until pink. Serve hot.

BROILED CLAMS
(Serves 4 to 6)

2 dozen clams, in shell
1/4 cup lemon juice
1 tablespoon rice wine *or* sherry
Salt
Lemon wedges

Combine lemon juice and wine, and rub on unopened clam shells (1 side only). Sprinkle heavily with salt. Place clams on tray, salted side up, and broil until clams open. Serve immediately with lemon wedges.

FOIL-WRAPPED CHICKEN
(Serves 4)

1/2 lb. chicken filet
1/4 lb. sliced smoked ham
1 tablespoon soy sauce
1 tablespoon salad oil
1 teaspoon cornstarch
1/4 teaspoon MSG
1/2 teaspoon salt
1 teaspoon sugar
1/4 teaspoon pepper
1 tablespoon rice wine *or* sherry
2 dozen aluminum foil squares, 5x5 inches
Oil for deep frying

Cut filet of chicken into 24 pieces. Cut slices of ham into 24 pieces. Mix chicken, soy sauce, salad oil, cornstarch, MSG, salt, sugar, pepper and sherry. Place chicken slice on square of foil and place slice of ham on top of it. Wrap as in illustration on page 49 for Egg Roll, but tuck in flap in step 4 to close envelope securely. Heat vegetable oil, about 1-inch deep, in frying pan and carefully drop foil-wrapped chicken packages into hot oil. Fry 1 to 2 minutes on each side. Drain and serve. Unwrap packages at table.

CRAB PUFFS
(Serves 6)

1 cup crab meat
1 3-oz. package cream cheese
1 teaspoon MSG
1/2 teaspoon salt
1/8 teaspoon white pepper
1 package won ton skin
1 egg, beaten

Mix all ingredients thoroughly, except won ton skins. Wrap meat mixture in won ton skin by placing 1 teaspoon of filling in center and folding outer corner towards opposite corner, forming a triangle. Brush edges with egg and seal. Fry in 370° fat. When brown, turn over and brown other side. Drain on paper towel.

MARINATED ABALONE CUBES
(Serves 4)

1 1-lb. can of abalone
1/4 cup soy sauce
2 tablespoons wine vinegar
1 teaspoon sugar
1/4 teaspoon minced ginger root
1/4 teaspoon hot mustard—*optional*
1/4 teaspoon sesame oil
Lettuce

Drain canned abalone and cut into 1-inch cubes. In bowl, toss abalone with other ingredients. Cover and chill in refrigerator for 1-1/2 to 2 hours. Skewer with cocktail picks and serve on bed of lettuce.

SHRIMP TOAST
(Serves 4)

1/2 lb. cooked shrimp, shelled and deveined
4 water chestnuts
1/4 teaspoon ginger powder
1 egg, lightly beaten
1 tablespoon cornstarch
1 tablespoon rice wine *or* sherry
1/4 teaspoon salt
4 slices white day-old bread
Oil for deep frying

Mince shrimp with water chestnuts. Combine with ginger powder, egg, cornstarch, wine and salt into a spreading paste consistency. Trim crust off bread and spread the shrimp paste over the slices. Cut these slices into triangles or squares. Heat oil in *wok*, or skillet, to 350°. Place several pieces of bread into oil, shrimpside down, with perforated spoon or ladle. Fry until light brown, turning over once. When uniformly brown, remove and drain on paper towel. Serve hot.

DEEP-FRIED FISH CAKES
(Serves 4)

1 lb. filet of pike, flounder or other white fish
1 teaspoon salt
1 teaspoon sugar
1 tablespoon soy sauce
2 tablespoons cornstarch
2 tablespoons ice water
1/4 teaspoon MSG
Oil for deep frying

Mince fish very fine. Blend with salt, sugar, soy sauce, cornstarch, water and MSG. Shape mixture into oblong cakes or balls, one tablespoonful each. In *wok*, or skillet, heat oil to 370°. Fry the cakes or balls, turning once or twice, until golden brown. Drain on paper towel.

FISH ROLLS
(Serves 4)

1/4 lb. halibut or sole
2 teaspoons sugar
3 tablespoons clam juice
1 tablespoon soy sauce
2 tablespoons rice wine *or* sherry
1/2 teaspoon salt
1 teaspoon oil
5 eggs, beaten
1 tablespoon cooking oil

Mince fish finely. Combine with sugar, clam juice, soy sauce, wine or sherry, salt and 1 teaspoon oil. Beat the eggs in a bowl and blend with fish mixture. In *wok*, or skillet, heat 1 tablespoon oil and pour in a thin layer of fish-egg batter. Brown on both sides then place on open napkin or paper towel. Roll into shape of small "jelly rolls" and let stand 5 minutes. Cut into 2-inch lengths.

CHICKEN WINGS STEWED IN WINE SAUCE
(Serves 4)

8 chicken wings
1/4 cup rice wine *or* sherry
1/2 cup soy sauce
2 tablespoons sugar
1 cup water
1 clove garlic, peeled and mashed
2 1/2-inch slices ginger root
1 full clove star anise
3-4 sprigs Chinese parsley—*optional*
Fresh lettuce leaves—*optional*

Cut off and discard small wing tips, and cut wings in two. In deep saucepan, combine all ingredients, except parsley and lettuce. Bring liquid to a boil. Lower heat and simmer, covered, 20 minutes. Uncover and continue to simmer 10 minutes, turning wings occasionally to get an even color. Drain (liquid can be refrigerated and reused) chicken wings and serve hot or cold. Arrange them on a bed of lettuce and garnish with parsley.

soups 湯

For many poor Chinese families, soups have always offered a complete meal in a bowl. And, because there is such an emphasis on soup *eating* in most Chinese homes and restaurants, soup *making* has been developed into quite a remarkable culinary art.

In recent years, processed soups have become very popular. However, the inclusion of preservatives in canned, dehydrated or frozen soups leaves a whole lot to be desired. That "certain something" having to do with taste and wholesomeness, can only be found in naturally made soups—particularly Chinese-style soups!

quick-boiled soups

The quick-boiled soups are a delight to make. They are simple, refreshing, nutritious and compatible with any Chinese dish. They are a great pick-me-up or snack. Generally, chicken bones or parts, pork bones and meat are used as a base for the soup, which takes only 15 to 20 minutes in a *wok* or soup kettle. By cooking vegetables in the soup, Chinese style, all the vitamins and minerals will be retained in the stock. Here's an example of what can be accomplished with a minimum of ingredients and expenditure: If pork and chicken wings are included on the dinner menu; get a few pork chops, trim away the pork bones and the tips of the chicken wings. Use these as the basic ingredients in your soup stock.

long-simmered soups

The heavy, long-simmered Chinese soups are desirable because of their textures and because of the wonderful blend of flavors produced by this slow cooking process.

Try some of these recipes. You'll find them rich, flavorful and satisfying.

BASIC CHICKEN SOUP
(Serves 6 to 7)

1/4 lb. chicken (or backs and necks of 2 chickens)
5 Chinese mushrooms, presoaked one hour
1 tablespoon *chung choy* (preserved turnips), finely chopped
1/2 teaspoon salt
6 cups water

In deep saucepan or soup kettle, combine all ingredients. Bring to boil. Then lower heat and simmer 1 hour. Take out chicken and pick meat off bones, Shred chicken meat and return to soup. Simmer another half hour.

BASIC PORK SOUP
(Serves 6 to 7)

1/4 lb. pork, sliced into pieces about 2 x 1/2 x 1/4 inches
1 tablespoon soy sauce
1/2 teaspoon salt
1 tablespoon *chung choy* (preserved turnips)
4 Chinese mushrooms, presoaked one hour
6 cups water

In deep saucepan or soup kettle, combine all ingredients. Bring to boil, then simmer 45 minutes.

BASIC MINCED PORK SOUP
(Serves 6 to 8)

1/4 lb. pork butt, minced
1 teaspoon soy sauce
1/2 teaspoon salt
3 teaspoons oil
6 cups boiling water

Marinate pork 1 hour in soy sauce, salt and 1 teaspoon oil. In deep saucepan or soup kettle, heat remaining oil and sauté pork until light brown. Add water. Bring to boil. Lower heat and simmer 45 minutes.

Variations of Basic Soups
(Serve 4 to 6)

WATERCRESS

1 bunch watercress, washed and cleaned, cut in 2-inch pieces
4 cups any basic soup stock

In deep saucepan or soup kettle, bring soup to boil. Add watercress to soup. Lower heat and simmer for 5 minutes.

SPINACH

1 bunch spinach
1/8 teaspoon garlic powder
4 cups basic soup (pork or minced pork)

In deep saucepan or soup kettle, bring soup to boil. Wash and separate spinach leaves. Add spinach and garlic powder to soup. Lower heat and simmer 3 minutes uncovered. Stir occasionally.

CHINESE CABBAGE (NAPA)

3/4 lb. Chinese cabbage leaves, cut in approximately 2-inch squares
4 cups any basic soup

In deep saucepan or soup kettle, bring soup to boil. Add Chinese cabbage. Lower heat and simmer 10 minutes.

PEAS

1 cup frozen peas
4 cups any basic soup
1 egg, beaten

In deep saucepan or soup kettle, bring soup to boil. Slowly add peas and simmer 5 minutes. Bring soup to active boil, slowly add egg. Cook, stirring for another minute.

LETTUCE

1 medium head lettuce, coarsely shredded
4 cups any basic soup
1 egg, beaten

In deep saucepan or soup kettle, bring soup to boil. Add lettuce. Lower heat and simmer 4 minutes. Bring to active boil. Add egg and cook, stirring for another minute.

CELERY AND CARROT

1/2 cup diced celery
1/2 cup diced carrots
4 cups any basic soup

In deep saucepan or soup kettle, bring soup to boil. Add carrots and celery. Lower heat and simmer 30 minutes.

CORN

3/4 cup whole kernel or creamed corn (canned)
4 cups any basic soup
1 egg, beaten

In deep saucepan or soup kettle, bring corn and soup to boil, stirring occasionally. Lower heat and simmer 5 minutes. Bring to active boil. Mix in egg, stirring actively. Cook 1 minute.

FUZZY MELON

1 medium fuzzy melon
4 cups any basic soup
1 egg, beaten

Scrape off skin of melon. Then quarter lengthwise and slice into 1/4-inch pieces. In deep saucepan or soup kettle, bring soup to boil. Add melon slices. Cook 2 minutes. Bring to active boil. Add egg, stirring, and cook additional 1 minute.

CHINESE MUSHROOM

12 dried Chinese mushrooms
4 cups basic chicken soup

Soak mushrooms overnight. Save liquid. In deep saucepan or soup kettle, combine basic soup, mushrooms and mushroom liquid. (Be careful not to pour in sediment, if any.) Bring to boil. Lower heat and simmer 30 minutes.

SEAWEED

1/8 lb. dried seaweed
4 cups any basic soup
1 egg, beaten

Soak seaweed in water 2 hours. Rinse under slowly running tap water, removing sand, etc. In deep saucepan or soup kettle, bring soup to boil. Add seaweed and simmer for 5 minutes. Add egg, stirring, and cook additional 1 minute.

MUSTARD GREENS

1/2 lb. Chinese mustard greens, washed and cut in 2-inch squares
4 cups basic pork soup
1 teaspoon sliced ginger

In deep saucepan or soup kettle, bring soup to boil. Add ginger and cook 5 minutes. Add mustard greens and simmer actively additional 5 minutes.

SOYBEAN CURD

1 cake fresh soybean curd, cut into 1/8 x 1 x 1 inch pieces
4 cups any basic soup

In deep saucepan or soup kettle, combine soup and bean cake. Bring to boil.

BITTER MELON

2 medium bitter melons
4 cups basic pork or minced pork soup

Slice melons lengthwise. Remove seeds and fibers, and cut melon crosswise into 1/4-inch-thick pieces. In deep saucepan or soup kettle, bring soup to boil. Add melon. Reduce heat and simmer 30 minutes.

CHINESE OKRA

3 medium okra pods
4 cups any basic soup
1 egg, beaten

Scrape or cut off ridges over length of pods. Cut pods diagonally into 1/2-inch pieces. In deep saucepan or soup kettle, bring soup to boil. Add okra and simmer 3 minutes. Bring back to boil and add egg. Stir actively 1 minute.

WINTER MELON

1/2 lb. winter melon, cut into 1-inch cubes
4 cups any basic soup
1 egg, beaten

In deep saucepan or soup kettle, bring soup to boil with melon. Reduce heat and simmer 10 minutes. Bring to boil and add egg, stirring actively 1 minute.

MATRIMONY VINE SOUP

1-1/2 lb. bunch matrimony vines
4 cups basic pork or minced-pork soup
1 egg, beaten

Wash matrimony vines in sink. Pick off withered leaves, if any. Strip leaves off stems (in same direction or growth of small thorns). Rinse in colander. In deep saucepan or soup kettle, bring soup to boil. Add matrimony vine leaves. Boil 2 minutes. Add egg, stirring actively 1 minute.

CHICKEN EGG FLOWER SOUP
(Serves 4 to 6)

1/2 cup minced chicken
4 cups chicken broth
1/4 cup finely chopped water chestnuts
2 eggs, beaten

In deep saucepan, combine chicken, broth and water chestnuts. Boil and then simmer 5 minutes. Bring back to active boil and stir in eggs.

CHICKEN AND BARLEY SOUP
(Serves 4 to 6)

4 cups soup stock
1/2 cup boneless chicken, finely chopped
1/4 cup barley, soaked in cold water 15 minutes and drained
2 tablespoons water chestnuts, diced
2 tablespoons white mushrooms, diced
1/8 teaspoon MSG
Salt *to taste*
Pepper *to taste*
2 tablespoons cooked Virginia ham, chopped fine

In deep saucepan or soup kettle, bring the soup stock to a rolling boil. Add chicken, drained barley, water chestnuts and mushrooms, and bring to boil again. Lower heat and simmer 45 minutes. Add MSG, and salt and pepper to taste. Sprinkle ham on each serving.

CHICKEN GIBLET SOUP
(Serves 4 to 6)

1/2 lb. chicken livers, washed and cut into 1/2-inch pieces
1/4 lb. chicken gizzards, cut 1/8-inch slices lengthwise and scored
1 tablespoon soy sauce
1/4 teaspoon sugar
2 tablespoons oil
1 clove garlic, minced
2 teaspoons minced ginger root
4 cups chicken broth or water
1 lb. spinach, washed, drained and coarsely shredded
1 teaspoon salt
1/4 teaspoon MSG

Mix livers and gizzards with soy sauce, sugar, 1 tablespoon oil. Heat remaining oil in deep saucepan or soup kettle. Stir-fry garlic and ginger about 1/2 minute. Add broth or water and bring to a boil. Add livers and gizzards, and simmer 20 minutes. Bring to active boil. Add spinach, salt and MSG. Lower heat and simmer, uncovered, 3 minutes, stirring occasionally.

CHICKEN SOUP WITH NOODLES
(Serves 4 to 6)

3/4 lb. thin, round noodles
Boiling water
4 cups chicken broth
1 tablespoon soy sauce
1/2 teaspoon sugar
1 whole chicken breast, cooked, skinned, boned and sliced into thin strips
1 green onion, finely chopped

Cook noodles in boiling, unsalted, water until tender. Blanche noodles in cold water and drain. Divide into deep serving bowls. Pour broth, soy sauce and sugar into large saucepan or soup kettle. Bring to a boil. Add chicken and simmer 10 minutes. Pour hot soup over noodles in individual bowls. Garnish with green onion.

CHICKEN AND PEA SOUP
(Serves 4 to 6)

- 4 cups chicken broth
- 1 cup raw chicken meat, diced
- 6 black imported or fresh mushrooms, soaked 2 hours and diced
- 2 water chestnuts, peeled and diced
- 1/4 teaspoon salt
- 1 teaspoon soy sauce
- 1 cup green peas—fresh, canned or frozen

Pour broth into large saucepan or soup kettle and bring to a boil. Add the chicken, mushrooms, water chestnuts, salt and simmer 15 minutes. Add soy sauce and stir thoroughly. Add peas and bring to boil. Simmer 5 minutes.

CHICKEN SOUP WITH MIXED VEGETABLES
(Serves 4 to 6)

- 1/2 cup cooked chicken, diced
- 4 cups chicken broth, heated
- 1/4 cup sliced mushrooms
- 1/4 cup diced celery
- Oil for sautéing
- 1/4 cup diced water chestnuts
- 1/2 cup bean sprouts
- 1 egg, beaten

Sauté mushrooms and celery in oil for two minutes in deep saucepan or soup kettle. Add chicken, chicken broth, water chestnuts and bean sprouts. Simmer for ten minutes. Bring to active boiling point and stir in egg. Boil for 1 minute.

DRIED FUNGUS AND CHICKEN SOUP
(Serves 4 to 6)

4 cups soup stock
1/4 cup dried wood fungus
2 water chestnuts, peeled and diced
2 tablespoons bamboo shoots, diced
1/2 cup white chicken meat (cook approximately 10 minutes and dice)
1/2 cup pork, diced
1 teaspoon soy sauce
1/8 teaspoon MSG
Salt *to taste*
Pepper *to taste*

In deep saucepan or soup kettle bring soup to a boil. Soak dried wood fungus in warm water 30 minutes and rinse with cold water several times. Add the soaked dried wood fungus, water chestnuts and bamboo shoots, and boil about 20 minutes. Add the chicken, pork, soy sauce, MSG, salt and pepper, and bring to a boil. Simmer 10 minutes.

BLACK MUSHROOM DUCK SOUP
(Serves 6 to 8)

    1 whole duck, chopped into 4 pieces
    4 water chestnuts, peeled and chopped
    8 dry imported black mushrooms
    2 tablespoons soy sauce
    1 tablespoon sugar
    1/4 teaspoon MSG
    1/4 teaspoon salt
    1/8 teaspoon white pepper
    Pinch Chinese five-spices
    2 teaspoons rice wine
    Oil for deep frying
    12 cups soup stock

Cover mushrooms in warm water and soak for 15 minutes. Drain water and add to soup pot. Marinate mushrooms in mixture of soy sauce, sugar, MSG, salt, pepper, Chinese five-spices and rice wine. Use one-half mixture for mushrooms and spread the other half thinly over the duck. Fry the duck in deep oil until browned. In deep saucepan or soup kettle, bring soup stock to boil and add the duck, mushrooms, marinade and water chestnuts. Bring to a boil. Lower heat and simmer 1-1/2 hours.

DRIED LILY SOUP WITH MIXED MEATS
(Serves 6 to 8)

    6 cups soup stock
    1 cup shredded raw meat (use three kinds)—chicken, pork, beef, veal, ham, duck or liver
    3/4 cup dried lilies, soaked 15 minutes in warm water and rinsed
    2 chopped water chestnuts
    1/8 teaspoon MSG
    1 teaspoon soy sauce
    1/4 teaspoon salt
    6-8 eggs, poached individually

In deep saucepan or soup kettle, bring the soup stock to a boil. Add the meat, lilies and water chestnuts. Cook for 10 minutes. Add the MSG, soy sauce, salt and pepper, and stir. Serve floating single poached egg in each portion.

MUSTARD GREEN SOUP
(Serves 4 to 6)

1/4 lb. fresh pork shoulder, sliced in 1/8 x 1/2 x 2-inch pieces
1 1/2-inch slice fresh ginger root
1/2 teaspoon salt
1 teaspoon peanut oil
4 cups water
1-1/2 cups mustard greens coarsely shredded

Combine pork, ginger, salt, peanut oil and water in large saucepan or soup kettle. Bring to boil. Cover and simmer 15 minutes. Add mustard greens. Cook 3 minutes or until greens are tender.

SPINACH AND EGG SOUP
(Serves 4 to 6)

3 cups beef broth
1 cup clam juice
2 cups spinach, coarsely chopped
2 eggs
1/4 teaspoon salt
1 teaspoon soy sauce
1 scallion, finely chopped

In deep saucepan or soup kettle, combine beef broth and clam juice. Bring to boil. Add spinach and simmer 5 minutes. Beat eggs together with salt and soy sauce. Bring soup to boil. Add eggs, stirring actively. Cook 1 minute. Garnish with scallions.

CHINESE CABBAGE SOUP
(Serves 4 to 6)

1 small head Chinese cabbage *(napa)*, coarsely shredded
1/4 lb. raw pork
1 teaspoon soy sauce
1 teaspoon cornstarch
1 teaspoon sugar
2 teaspoons oil
1 teaspoon minced ginger root
4 cups chicken broth or water
1 teaspoon salt

Trim fat and cut pork into thin strips. Mix with soy sauce, cornstarch and sugar. Heat oil in deep saucepan or soup kettle. Add ginger root and cook for 1 minute. Add broth or water and salt. Cover and bring to boil. Add pork mixture and simmer 15 minutes. Remove cover, bring soup to boil and add cabbage. Simmer, uncovered, for 5 minutes, stirring occasionally.

CLEAR FRESH BEAN CURD SOUP
(Serves 4 to 6)

1 lb. lean pork butt, cut into 2-inch chunks
4 large Chinese mushrooms, presoaked 2 hours
4 dried red dates, presoaked 4 hours
1 piece dried tangerine peel, presoaked 2 hours
2 cakes fresh bean curd, quartered
4 cups water

In deep saucepan or soup kettle, combine all ingredients. Bring to boil. Reduce heat and simmer 2 hours.

FRESH BEAN CURD AND CABBAGE SOUP
(Serves 4)

1/2 lb. lean raw pork, sliced
1/2 teaspoon salt
4 cups chicken soup or water
2 cakes fresh bean curd, each cut into 10 pieces
1 cup Chinese cabbage *(napa)*, coarsely shredded
1/4 cup water chestnuts, finely sliced

In deep saucepan or soup kettle, combine pork, salt and soup or water. Bring to boil, then simmer 20 minutes. Add bean curd, Chinese cabbage, water chestnuts. Simmer 10 minutes.

DRIED CHINESE CHARD SOUP
(Serves 6 to 8)

1-1/2 lbs. pork bones or 1 lb. pork butt
1/8 lb. dried Chinese chard, soaked overnight
1 piece dried tangerine peel, approximately 2-inches square
8 cups water
2 cakes fresh bean curd, quartered
Salt *to taste*

Wash Chinese chard several times and cut into 2-inch lengths. In deep saucepan or soup kettle, combine pork bones, Chinese chard, tangerine peel, and water. Bring to boil, then simmer 1-1/2 hours. (If pork butt is used, remove and cut into chunks after cooking.) Add fresh bean curd and simmer 10 minutes. Cut up pork into bite-size pieces. Return to soup and salt to taste.

LOTUS ROOT SOUP
(Serves 6 to 8)

    1 dried cuttlefish, soaked overnight
    1-1/2 lb. fresh lotus root
    2 lbs. pork neck bones or shank
    4 dried Chinese mushrooms, presoaked 2 hours
    3 dried red dates, presoaked 2 hours
    2 dried scallops, presoaked 3 hours—save liquid
    8 cups water
    Salt *to taste*

Remove cuttle bone from cuttlefish and cut cuttlefish into small pieces. Wash and scrub lotus root. Cut lengthwise, then across into 1/4-inch thick slices. (If dried lotus root used, use about 1/2 lb.) Combine all ingredients and bring to boil. Simmer 4 to 5 hours. Salt to taste.

BEEF SOUP WITH CHINESE TURNIPS
(Serves 4 to 6)

    1 cup beef short ribs, boned
    1 tablespoon oil
    1 teaspoon soy sauce
    2 teaspoons rice wine
    6 cups soup stock
    1 cup Chinese turnips, cut into 1-1/2-inch cubes
    4 water chestnuts, thinly sliced
    1 tablespoon chopped onion
    1 1/4-inch slice fresh ginger
    1/4 teaspoon MSG
    Salt *to taste*
    Pepper *to taste*

Cut beef into 1-inch square pieces and cook in oil in deep saucepan or soup kettle until browned. Add soy sauce and rice wine, and cook 2 minutes. Then cover pan and let cook over low heat another 10 minutes. Add soup stock and bring to a boil. Lower heat and simmer 60 minutes. Add turnips, water chestnuts, onion and ginger, and bring to a boil. Lower heat and simmer another 30 minutes. Season with MSG, salt and pepper. Stir 1 minute.

WATERCRESS SOUP
(Serves 4 to 6)

1/2 lb. pork
1 teaspoon soy sauce
4 cups beef broth *or* water
1 bunch watercress
1 egg, beaten

Dice the pork into approximately 1/4 x 1/2 x 1-inch pieces. Mix with soy sauce and let stand for 15 minutes. In deep pot or soup kettle, bring broth or water to a boil. Add pork and soy sauce. Cook over medium heat for 10 minutes. Add watercress and cook uncovered for 5 minutes. Stir in eggs until set.

CLEAR WATERCRESS SOUP
(Serves 4)

1-1/2 lbs. pork bones
1 bunch watercress, washed and cleaned
4 Chinese mushrooms, presoaked 2 hours and sliced
2 dried scallops, presoaked 2 hours and chopped
1 piece dried tangerine peel, presoaked 2 hours
1/2 teaspoon salt
6 cups water

In deep saucepan or soup kettle, combine all ingredients. Bring to boil. Lower heat and simmer 2 hours.

QUICK-COOKED WATERCRESS SOUP
(Serves 4)

    4 cups chicken broth
    1/4 teaspoon salt
    3/4 teaspoon sugar
    2 teaspoons soy sauce
    2-4 paper-thin slices fresh ginger root
    1 large bunch watercress, stems removed and broken into sprigs
    2 tablespoons finely sliced green onions

In deep saucepan or soup kettle, combine the chicken broth, salt, sugar, soy sauce, ginger. Simmer 15 minutes. Bring to full boil. Add watercress and green onions. Cover, reduce heat and simmer 5 minutes.

LOBSTER AND WATERCRESS SOUP
(Serves 6 to 8)

    2 lobster tails
    6 cups beef broth
    1 tablespoon soy sauce
    1 cup watercress

Split lobster lengthwise. Remove meat from body and claws and slice into bite-size pieces. In deep pot, bring broth and soy sauce to boil. Add the lobster and cook over low heat 10 minutes. Stir in the watercress and cook 5 minutes.

FISH AND VEGETABLE SOUP
(Serves 4 to 6)

8 dried mushrooms—Chinese, if available
3/4 cup warm water
1/2 lb. white-meat fish
2 cups beef broth
2 cups clam juice
1 cup coarsely chopped spinach
2 scallions, thinly sliced
1 teaspoon soy sauce
1/2 teaspoon salt
4 thin slices lemon rind

Wash the mushrooms and soak in warm water 20 minutes. Drain, reserving the water. Slice the mushrooms. Cut the fish into narrow slices. In deep saucepan or soup kettle, bring the broth, clam juice and the mushroom water to a boil. Add the fish and mushrooms and cook over low heat 8 minutes. Stir in spinach, scallions, soy sauce and salt. Cook 4 minutes. Serve with slices of lemon rind.

FISH BALL SOUP
(Serves 4 to 6)

1/2 lb. sole filet
1/2 lb. shrimp, shelled and deveined
1 scallion
1 teaspoon soy sauce
1/4 teaspoon powdered ginger
1 teaspoon cornstarch
1 teaspoon oil
2 cups clam broth
2 cups beef broth
1 cup shredded spinach

Mince together sole, shrimp and scallion. Blend with soy sauce, ginger, cornstarch and oil. Divide the mixture and roll into marble-sized balls. In deep saucepan or soup kettle, bring soup to boil. Carefully immerse fish balls into soup. Simmer 10 minutes. Bring soup to boil. Add spinach and simmer, uncovered, 5 minutes. Stir occasionally.

SHRIMP SOUP
(Serves 4 to 6)

1/2 lb. shrimp, shelled and deveined
1/4 teaspoon salt
1/2 teaspoon sugar
1 teaspoon cornstarch
1 teaspoon water
2 cups clam juice
2 cups beef broth
2 teaspoons sliced mushrooms
1/4 cup green peas
1 teaspoon soy sauce

Mince shrimp very finely. Combine with salt, sugar, cornstarch and water. Roll into marble-sized balls. In deep saucepan or soup kettle, combine clam juice and beef broth and bring to a boil. Carefully drop shrimp balls into soup. Simmer 15 minutes. Add mushrooms, green peas and soy sauce. Bring to boil. Simmer 5 minutes.

SHRIMP AND CABBAGE SOUP
(Serves 4 to 6)

1/2 lb. raw shrimp, shelled, deveined and chopped
2 teaspoons oil
2 cups Chinese celery cabbage *(napa)* or American green cabbage, shredded or cut into 2 inch square pieces
1/2 cup sliced water chestnuts
1-1/2 teaspoons salt
6 cups water
4 scallions, finely chopped

Sauté shrimp in oil in saucepan or soup kettle for 3 minutes. Add cabbage, water chestnuts, salt and water. Bring to boil. Cover and simmer for 15 minutes (or until cabbage is tender but crisp). Garnish with scallions.

SHRIMP AND CORN SOUP
(Serves 4 to 6)

1/2 lb. raw shrimp, shelled, deveined and diced
2 cups bottled clam juice
3/4 cup thinly sliced onions
1 large garlic clove, minced
2 tablespoons oil
1/2 teaspoon freshly ground black pepper
1/2 cup canned whole-kernel corn
2 cups water
1/2 cup shredded Chinese mustard greens *or* spinach

Sauté onions and garlic in oil for 1 minute in large pot or soup kettle. Add shrimp and sauté for 2 minutes. Add clam juice, corn, pepper, and water. Bring to a boil. Then simmer for 10 minutes. Add mustard greens, or spinach, and cook 2 more minutes.

CRAB AND CREAMED CORN SOUP
(Serves 4 to 6)

4 cups chicken or pork soup stock
1 cup crab meat, very finely chopped
1 can #1-1/2 cream-style corn
2 tablespoons cooked Virginia ham finely chopped
2 tablespoons water chestnuts, peeled and finely chopped
1/4 teaspoon MSG
Salt *to taste*
Pepper *to taste*
1 cup cream *or* milk
1 egg, well beaten

In deep saucepan or soup kettle, bring soup stock to boil. Add crab meat and cook 5 minutes. Add cream-style corn. Stir. Then add ham, water chestnuts, MSG, salt and pepper. Simmer 5 minutes. Slowly add the cream, or milk, and stir thoroughly. Bring to active boil and stir in egg. Cook 1 minute, stirring.

PARSLEY CLAM SOUP
(Serves 4 to 6)

24 clams in shell
2 cups chicken broth
2 cups clam juice
3 tablespoons finely chopped onions
2 tablespoons minced parsley
1 tablespoon soy sauce
1 tablespoon rice wine *or* sherry

Scrub the clams and wash thoroughly. Bring the broth and clam juice to a boil. Drop the clams and onions into soup. Cook over medium heat until clams open. Stir in the parsley, soy sauce and wine. Serve in deep plates.

CLAM AND BEEF SOUP
(Serves 4)

24 clams in shell
1/2 lb. ground beef
2 tablespoons oil
2 tablespoons ground sesame seed
1 garlic clove, minced
1 tablespoon soy sauce
4 cups water
1/8 teaspoon dried ground chili peppers

Thoroughly scrub clams. Heat oil in deep saucepan or soup kettle and sauté beef until brown. Add sesame seeds, garlic, soy sauce, water and chili peppers. Bring to boil. Then simmer over low heat approximately 30 minutes. Add clams. Cook until clams open.

Note: You can substitute 2 cans minced clams. Cook 5 minutes.

SPINACH, CLAM AND EGG SOUP
(Serves 4 to 6)

2 cups beef broth
2 cups clam juice
2 cups coarsely chopped spinach
1/4 cup finely chopped scallions
1 egg
1/4 teaspoon salt
1 teaspoon soy sauce

In deep saucepan or soup kettle, bring beef broth and clam juice to a boil. Add spinach and scallions. Let simmer for 4 minutes. Beat the egg, salt and soy sauce together. Stir into the soup. Cook 1 minute.

ABALONE AND CHICKEN SOUP
(Serves 6 to 8)

1/2 lb. coarsely chopped chicken
4 Chinese mushrooms, presoaked 2 hours and thinly sliced
1/2 1-lb. can abalone, thinly sliced
4 water chestnuts, peeled and finely sliced
1/2 teaspoon salt
6 cups water

In deep saucepan or soup kettle, combine chicken, mushrooms, salt and water. Bring to boil. Reduce heat and simmer 30 minutes. Bring to boil. Add abalone and water chestnuts. Simmer 2 minutes.

ABALONE SOUP WITH PORK BALLS
(Serves 4 to 6)

3/4 lb. finely minced pork butt
4 Chinese mushrooms, presoaked 2 hours in 1 cup water and thinly sliced—save water
1/2 1-lb. can abalone, thinly sliced
1 teaspoon cornstarch
1 tablespoon soy sauce
1 teaspoon oil
1/2 teaspoon salt
4 cups chicken broth

Mix together pork, cornstarch, soy sauce, oil and salt. Roll into balls about 1/2-inch in diameter. In deep saucepan or soup kettle, combine mushrooms, mushroom water and broth. Bring to boil and simmer 15 minutes. Slowly add pork balls. Bring to boil. Lower heat and simmer 20 minutes. Bring to boil again and add abalone. Cook 2 more minutes.

DRIED OYSTER AND BEAN CURD SOUP
(Serves 6 to 8)

1/2 lb. pork butt, cut into 1-inch bite-size pieces
6 Chinese mushrooms, presoaked 2 hours
4 dried oysters, rinsed then soaked overnight—add fluid, except for bottom sediment, to soup
2 dried red dates, soaked overnight
6 cups water
1/4 teaspoon salt
1 cake fresh bean curd, cut into 16 pieces

In deep saucepan or soup kettle, combine pork, mushrooms, oysters, red dates and water. Bring to boil. Lower heat and simmer 3 hours. In separate pot, boil bean curd until soft. Blanche with cold water. Bring soup to boil. Add bean curd, then simmer 10 minutes. Add salt to taste.

SHARK'S FIN SOUP
(Serves 4 to 6)

1/4 lb. shark fin—dried cake type, presoaked 3 hours
2 1/4-inch-thick slices ginger root, crushed
1/4 cup rice wine *or* sherry
6 cups chicken soup
2 tablespoons cooked chicken meat, diced or shredded
1/4 teaspoon salt
1 egg, beaten
2 tablespoons cooked ham, finely chopped

Place presoaked shark fin in pot. Cover with cold water. Bring water to boiling point. Let stand 60 seconds. Strain and repeat process 2 or 3 times. Marinate shark fin in ginger root and wine for 1 hour. Remove ginger. In deep saucepan or soup kettle, bring soup to boil. Add shark fin. Reduce heat and simmer 4 hours. Bring to boil. Stir in chicken meat, salt and egg. Cook 1 minute. Garnish with ham.

PORK MEATBALL SOUP
(Serves 4 to 6)

1/2 lb. raw pork, minced
1 egg
1/4 cup very finely chopped scallions
1/2 teaspoon salt
1/4 teaspoon pepper
1-1/2 teaspoons soy sauce
4 cups chicken broth

Mix pork with eggs, scallions, salt, pepper and soy sauce. Divide and shape pork into 12 small meatballs. Bring broth, or water, to a boil and carefully drop in meatballs. Cover and simmer 45 minutes.

HOT AND SOUR SZECHWAN SOUP
(Serves 4)

1/2 lb. raw pork, minced
4 cups chicken broth
1 teaspoon salt
1 teaspoon soy sauce
1/4 cup finely chopped bamboo shoots
3 Chinese mushrooms, presoaked and finely sliced
1/4 cup white vinegar
1/4 teaspoon crushed red peppers
1 cake fresh bean curd, cut into 16ths
2 tablespoons cornstarch, mixed to paste with cold water
1 egg, beaten
1/4 teaspoon sesame oil
1 green onion, finely chopped

In deep saucepan, combine pork, chicken broth, salt, soy sauce, bamboo shoots, mushrooms, vinegar and peppers. Bring to boil. Then simmer, covered, 20 minutes. Add bean curd and simmer 3 minutes. Stir in cornstarch mixture. Simmer until cornstarch sets. Bring soup to active boil and stir in egg. Add sesame oil. Garnish with scallion.

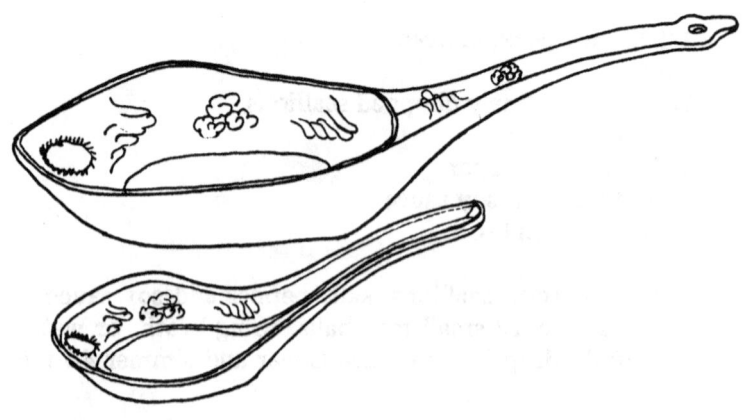

PORK AND BEAN CAKE SOUP
(Serves 4 to 6)

4 cups chicken broth
1 tablespoon soy sauce
1 teaspoon sugar
1/4 lb. lean fresh pork
2 dried mushrooms, soaked 2 hours in 1/4 cup water —
   save liquid *or* 1 4-oz. can sliced mushrooms
1 chopped green onion
1 cake fresh bean curd

Combine broth, soy sauce and sugar in a deep saucepan or soup kettle. Cut the pork into thin strips about 1/4-inch thick and 2 inches long. Rinse and finely slice mushrooms. Bring broth to boil. Add pork, mushrooms and their liquid, onion and bean cake. Simmer about 30 minutes.

HAM AND VEGETABLE SOUP
(Serves 6 to 8)

8 cups clear ham bone, chicken and vegetable soup
   stock
1/2 cup tomato wedges
1/2 cup shredded Chinese cabbage
1/2 cup diced green pepper
1/2 cup diced onions
1/2 cup diced celery
1/2 cup diced water chestnuts
1/2 cup sliced fresh mushrooms
1/2 cup fresh, frozen or canned peas
1 cup diced ham
1/2 teaspoon MSG
2 teaspoons soy sauce
Salt *to taste*
Pepper *to taste*

Bring soup stock to boil. Add vegetables and ham.. Simmer for 8 minutes. Add MSG, soy sauce, salt and pepper, and stir thoroughly.

WON TON SOUP
(Serves 4 to 6)

2 dozen filled but uncooked won ton
Boiling water
4 cups chicken broth
1/2 teaspoon sesame oil—*optional*
1-1/2 teaspoons soy sauce
2 green onions, finely chopped

Drop filled won ton into deep saucepan or soup kettle of boiling water. Cook 6 at a time to prevent their sticking together. After they rise to the top of the water, simmer 4 minutes. Pour them into colander. Rinse in warm water and drain. In deep saucepan or soup kettle, combine chicken broth, sesame oil and soy sauce. Bring to a boil. Drop in the won ton and cook 1 minute. Garnish with green onions.

WINTER MELON SOUP WITH HAM AND CHICKEN
(Serves 4 to 6)

4 cups soup stock
1 cup winter melon, cut into 1/2-inch cubes
1/2 cup diced chicken
1/2 cup cooked Virginia ham, diced
2 tablespoons water chestnuts, peeled and diced
1/4 cup white mushrooms, diced
1/4 teaspoon MSG
1 teaspoon soy sauce
Salt *to taste*
Pepper *to taste*
1/8 teaspoon sesame oil—*optional*

Bring the soup stock to a boil. Add the winter melon and return to a boil. Lower heat and simmer for 1 hour. Add the chicken, ham, chestnuts and mushrooms, and cook for 20 minutes. Add MSG, soy sauce, salt, pepper and sesame oil. Stir and serve.

WHOLE WINTER MELON SOUP WITH DICED MEATS
(Serves 8 to 10)

1 whole winter melon, about 10 lbs.
2 cups raw chicken meat, diced
2 cups raw pork butt, diced
1 cup ham, diced
8 dried Chinese mushrooms, soaked 2 hours and diced—save liquid and add to soup
1/2 cup water chestnuts, peeled and diced
1/2 cup bamboo shoots, diced
1/2 cup peanuts, blanched
1/2 cup chicken gizzards, diced
1 medium-sized piece dried tangerine peel
2 teaspoons soy sauce
Salt *to taste*
8 cups chicken-soup stock

Wash and scrub winter melon. Cut off top to make lid (about 2-1/2-inches). Remove melon seeds and fibers. Place melon upright in large bowl or container and place in pot large enough so melon can be covered completely. Sauté all meats with mushrooms, water chestnuts, bamboo shoots and peanuts for 3 minutes, and then place inside melon. Add additional water, if necessary, to bring liquid to 1/2-inch of top. Add tangerine peel, soy sauce and salt. Place lid on melon. Add sufficient water to bottom of pot for steaming whole melon. Bring water to a boil. Place cover on pot and simmer 2-1/2 to 3 hours. Occasionally stir contents of whole melon. To serve, remove lid of melon, carefully scoop out melon meat and include with other ingredients. For complete enjoyment, bring whole melon to dining table.

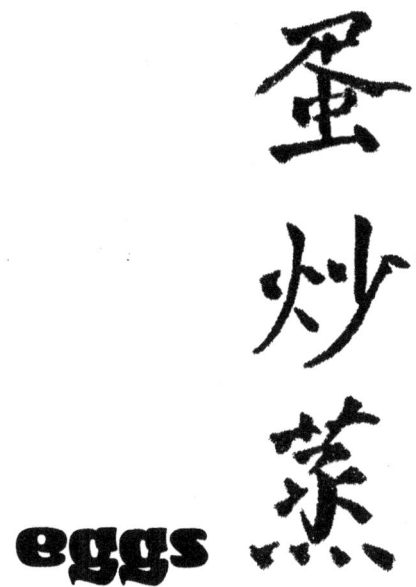

eggs

Preserved, boiled, poached, stir-fried, scrambled, panfried, deep fried, steamed, simmered, used in *foo yong* patties, custards, or simply as a garnish, eggs have been adapted to every type of Chinese dish.

For the Chinese, eggs are not confined to the breakfast menu. Their preparation in Chinese dishes is quite easy and, in most instances, very imaginative. Inasmuch as eggs are readily available, reasonable and easy to store, I always try to have a dozen or so on hand for quick nourishing snacks or that appetizing extra dish to fill out a menu. Egg dishes are the perfect addition when an unexpected extra guest or member of the family arrives at mealtime.

Generally, eggs are not cooked alone, but with a small amount of one or two ingredients that blend well together and delicately season the eggs. Like rice, eggs assume new personalities when prepared with small amounts of leftover meats and diced vegetables. And, believe it or not, we Chinese even eat them hard-boiled!

BASIC RECIPE FOR STIR-FRIED EGGS
(Serves 4)

6 eggs
1 teaspoon soy sauce
2 tablespoons oil
1/2 teaspoon salt
2 stalks scallion, finely chopped or slivered

Beat eggs well and blend in soy sauce. In *wok*, or skillet, heat oil. Add salt and scallions. Stir-fry few seconds. Reduce heat to medium. Add eggs, stir slowly with chopsticks or spatula until set. Serve.

STIR-FRIED EGGS WITH PORK AND MUSHROOMS
(Serves 4)

5 fresh eggs
1/4 lb. lean pork, minced
1/4 cup bamboo shoots, diced
4 dried mushrooms, presoaked and diced
1 teaspoon soy sauce
1/4 teaspoon MSG
1/4 teaspoon sesame oil
2 tablespoons oil
1/2 teaspoon salt

Beat eggs well, adding soy sauce, MSG and sesame oil. In *wok*, or skillet, heat oil and add salt, then pork. Stir-fry until pork no longer has pink coloring. Add bamboo shoots, mushrooms and stir-fry 1 minute. Reduce to medium heat and stir in eggs. Cook until eggs are firm.

THREE VARIETIES OF STEAMED EGGS
(Serves 4)

1 preserved 1,000-year-old egg
1 preserved salted egg
2 fresh eggs
1/4 cup soup stock
1/2 teaspoon salt
1 scallion, chopped

Remove covering from preserved egg; wash and boil for 2 minutes. Shell and dice. Remove covering from salted egg; wash, separate white from yolk and dice yolk. In bowl, beat 2 fresh eggs and combine well with all ingredients except scallion. Transfer to deep platter. Place platter on rack in *wok*, or deep pot, with 2 inches of water. Bring water to boil. Cover and steam 20 to 25 minutes. Test by inserting knife. If it comes out clean, remove from pot or *wok*. Garnish with scallions.

Variations for Stir-Fried Eggs
(Follow basic recipe on all following variations, adding eggs)

HAM

Add 1/2 cup finely diced ham. Stir-fry ham with scallions.

HAM AND ONIONS

Substitute 1/4 cup diced onion for scallions. Add 1/4 cup diced ham. Stir-fry onions and ham with salt until ham is slightly browned.

BACON AND HAM

Substitute 2 slices bacon for oil. Cut bacon crosswise into 1/4-inch pieces. Add 1/4 cup finely slivered ham. Fry bacon pieces until almost crisp. Add ham and scallions. Stir-fry with eggs.

SHRIMP

Add 1/2 cup cooked or raw shrimp, shelled, deveined, and chopped. Stir-fry shrimp with scallions and salt until pink.

SHRIMP AND WATER CHESTNUTS

Add 2 tablespoons water chestnuts, peeled and chopped to Shrimp variation above.

CRAB MEAT

Add 1/2 cup flaked crab meat. Stir-fry crab meat with scallions.

CRAB MEAT AND BAMBOO SHOOTS

Add 1/4 cup slivered bamboo shoots to Crab Meat variation.

DRIED BABY SHRIMP

Add 1/4 cup dried baby shrimp, presoaked 1 hour. Drain well (save liquid). Stir-fry shrimp with scallions for 1 minute. Add 1 tablespoon soaking liquid to eggs before stir-frying with shrimp.

DRIED MUSHROOMS

Add 1/2 cup Chinese dried mushrooms, presoaked and sliced. Drain. Add 1-1/4-inch slice ginger root, minced. Stir-fry mushrooms, ginger root and scallions together.

DRIED MUSHROOMS AND WATER CHESTNUTS

Add 1/4 cup water chestnuts, peeled and sliced to DRIED MUSHROOM variation.

OYSTER SAUCE

When eggs are almost set in basic recipe, stir in 1 tablespoon oyster sauce. Place eggs in dish or bowl and sprinkle another tablespoon oyster sauce over them. Garnish with Chinese parsley.

GREEN PEAS AND BABY ONIONS

Add 1 package frozen green peas and onions, thawed. Stir-fry with scallions. Cover and simmer 3 minutes.

Eggs

GREEN PEAS, ONIONS AND HAM

Add 1/2 cup green peas, 1/4 cup diced onion, and 1/4 cup finely diced ham. Stir-fry scallions, onions and ham for a few seconds. Add peas, stir-fry to mix. Cover and simmer 3 minutes.

BELL PEPPER, ONION, HAM

Add 1 bell pepper, seeds removed, rinsed and finely chopped, 1 medium onion, peeled and diced, and 1/4 cup ham, diced. Stir-fry ham, scallions, onion for a few seconds. Add bell pepper. Stir-fry to mix. Cover and simmer 2 minutes.

CHIPPED BEEF

Add 1/2 cup chipped beef, shredded. Stir-fry with scallions a few seconds.

BASIC RECIPE FOR EGG FOO YUNG
(Serves 4)

6 eggs
1/2 teaspoon salt
1/4 teaspoon MSG
1 teaspoon soy sauce
3/4 cup cooked meat
1-1/2 cups bean sprouts, chopped
2 tablespoons oil
1 scallion, chopped, for garnish

Beat eggs and mix in salt, MSG, soy sauce. Fold in the meat and sprouts. Heat oil in *wok*, or skillet, and drop 3 tablespoons of egg mixture in pan to form foo yung patty. When bottom is brown, flip patty over and brown other side. Remove and keep warm. Repeat until you use up the egg mixture.

EGG FOO YUNG SAUCE
(Optional)

1 cup soup stock
1 teaspoon soy sauce
1/2 teaspoon salt
1/4 teaspoon MSG
1 tablespoon cornstarch
2 tablespoons water

Heat soup stock, soy sauce, salt and MSG. Mix cornstarch with water into a smooth paste and stir into soup stock until sauce thickens. Pour sauce over egg foo yung patties.

Variations For Egg Foo Yung

(Follow basic recipe on all following variations.)

CLAMS
3/4 cup raw or canned minced clams
1/4 cup finely slivered green onions
1 cup blanched bean sprouts

SHRIMP
3/4 cup cooked shrimp
1/2 cup finely chopped celery
1/4 cup finely chopped water chestnuts
1/2 cup chopped bean sprouts

BARBECUED PORK
3/4 cup finely slivered barbecue pork
1 scallion stalk, finely chopped
1/4 cup Chinese dried mushrooms, presoaked, drained and sliced
1 cup blanched bean sprouts

Eggs

CHICKEN AND BEAN SPROUTS

3/4 cup cooked white chicken meat, diced
1/2 cup sliced onions
1-1/2 cups blanched bean sprouts

CHICKEN AND FRESH MUSHROOMS

3/4 cup cooked white chicken, diced
1 cup fresh mushrooms, sliced
1/2 cup sliced onions

TURKEY MEAT

Substitute turkey for chicken in variation above.

CRAB

1 cup flaked crab meat
1 cup blanched bean sprouts
1 scallion, chopped
1 1/4-inch slice ginger root, minced

COOKED HAM

3/4 cup cooked ham slivered
1/4 cup bamboo shoots, slivered in 2-inch lengths
1 cup blanched bean sprouts

VEGETABLES ONLY

1 cup blanched bean sprouts
1/2 cup parboiled french-cut string beans
1/2 cup fresh mushrooms, sliced
1/4 cup chopped water chestnuts
1/4 cup sliced onions

STIR-FRIED FLOWERED EGGS
(Serves 4)

6 fresh eggs
1/4 cup slivered barbecued pork or cooked ham
1/4 cup Chinese dried mushrooms, presoaked, finely sliced
1/3 cup snow peas, trimmed and finely sliced
1/4 cup bamboo shoots, finely sliced
2 scallions, slivered 1-1/2-inch lengths
1/4 teaspoon MSG
2 teaspoon oil
1/2 teaspoon salt

Add MSG to eggs and beat. In *wok*, or skillet, heat oil. Add salt and pork or ham. Stir-fry a few seconds and add the rest of the ingredients, except the eggs. Stir-fry to mix and cook 3 minutes. Add eggs, stirring and cooking over medium heat until they are firm.

PRESERVED SALTED EGGS STEAMED WITH PORK
(Serves 4)

1 lb. pork, minced
2 salted eggs
2 fresh eggs
1 teaspoon salt
1/4 teaspoon MSG
1/4 cup water
1 tablespoon soy sauce
1 scallion, chopped

Remove protective brine layer from salted eggs. Wash eggs, crack open and separate whites from yolks. In bowl, slightly beat 2 fresh eggs and mix well with pork, salted egg whites, salt, MSG, water and soy sauce. Transfer to deep platter and shape into patty covering platter. Flatten salted egg yolks with cleaver and place yolks on meat patty. (You may flatten yolks. dice and scatter over patty.) Place platter on rack in *wok*, or deep pot, with 2 inches water. Bring water to boil. Cover and steam 25 to 30 minutes. Garnish with chopped scallion.

CRISP FRIED EGGS WITH OYSTER SAUCE
(Serves 4)

6 eggs
2 tablespoons oil
8 teaspoonsful oyster sauce
1 scallion, finely chopped
2 cups cooked rice

In *wok*, or skillet, heat the oil. Fry eggs individually over medium heat until crisp around edges as desired. Sprinkle 8 teasponsful oyster sauce over eggs. Place eggs on platter and garnish with scallion, or place directly on bed of rice in bowl.

DEEP-FRIED EGGS WITH OYSTER SAUCE
(Serves 4 to 6)

6 eggs
2 tablespoons oyster sauce
1/3 cup peanut oil

Heat peanut oil in *wok*, or skillet, to 350°. Fry eggs one at a time until light brown around edges. Place deep-fried eggs on plate of lettuce. Pour oyster sauce over eggs and serve hot.

BASIC STEAMED EGGS
(Serves 4)

3-4 eggs
1 teaspoon rice wine *or* sherry
1 teaspoon oil
1/2 teaspoon salt
1/2 teaspoon sugar
1/4 teaspoon MSG
3/4 cup soup stock
1 teaspoon soy sauce *or* oyster sauce
1 scallion, finely chopped

In deep, heat-proof bowl, lightly beat eggs and combine with wine, oil, salt, sugar, MSG. Gently stir in warm soup stock. Place bowl on rack in deep pot with 2 inches water. Bring water to boil. Cover pot and steam eggs 20 to 30 minutes. Test by inserting knife blade. If clean on removal, preparation is cooked. Sprinkle soy sauce or oyster sauce over surface. Garnish with scallions.

Variations for Steamed Eggs

*(Singly or in combination,
add following to egg mixture before steaming.)*

MEAT

1/4 cup smoked ham, minced
1/4 cup Canadian bacon, finely chopped
1/2 cup chipped beef, chopped
2 Chinese sausages, finely sliced diagonally
1/2 cup roast pork, chopped
1/2 cup chicken, chopped
1/4 cup Italian sausage, chopped
1/4 cup Kosher salami, finely diced

SEAFOOD

2 tablespoons dried shrimp, presoaked and chopped
1/2 cup crab meat, shredded
1/2 cup lobster, shredded
1/2 cup oysters, chopped
1/2 cup clams, chopped—substitute clam broth for soup stock
3 dried scallops, soaked and shredded
1/2 cup fresh or cooked shrimp, finely chopped
1/2 cup finnan haddie, flaked

VEGETABLES

1/2 cup fresh mushrooms, chopped
1/2 cup Chinese parsley, chopped
1/2 cup water chestnuts, peeled and chopped
1/4 cup Chinese chives, cut in 1/4-inch lengths

pork

I can remember a rumor that circulated in San Francisco when I was young, that the price of pork for all of California was set and controlled in Chinatown. While there may never have been any foundation in fact to that rumor, it *is* true that enormous quantities of pork are consumed in the homes and restaurants of Chinatowns everywhere.

Most of the Chinese in America have a great fondness for pork and use it generously, either alone or in combination with other meats, in many of their favorite dishes.

This appreciation for pork over other equally available American meats, such as beef and lamb, can be traced back to southern China where the pig was the most economically raised meat-producing animal.

In the following recipes, you will discover some of the versatility of pork and many of the delectable ways it can be prepared.

BRAISED PORK SHOULDER
(Serves 6)

1 6-lb. pork shoulder
2 cups water
1/4 cup rice wine *or* sherry
1 cup soy sauce
4 1/4-inch slices of ginger root, mashed
4 scallions
1 tablespoon sugar
Hot cooked rice

Wash pork and clean skin thoroughly. Place the meat, skinside up, in a heavy saucepan with the water. Cook at high heat. When water boils, pour the wine over pork; then the soy sauce. Place ginger root and scallions in the liquid. Cover, lower heat and simmer for 1 hour. Turn the meat and simmer for 1 hour more. Turn the meat again and add sugar. Cook for 30 minutes longer. The meat should be tender enough to give way with chopsticks. Serve in deep platter on a bed of steaming rice. If desired, thicken sauce with cornstarch and pour over meat.

BRAISED PORK SHOULDER
(Serves 3 to 4)

2 lbs. pork shoulder
2 tablespoons oil
1/4 cup soy sauce
2 1/4-inch slices fresh ginger root, mashed
3 scallions
1/4 cup rice wine *or* sherry
1-3/4 cups cold water
1 tablespoon brown sugar
1 tablespoon cornstarch

Heat oil in *wok*, or skillet. Brown pork on all sides. Add all ingredients, except brown sugar, cornstarch and 1/4 cup water. Cover and simmer 1-1/2 hours, turning occasionally. Add brown sugar. Simmer another 1/2 hour, or until meat is tender. Remove meat and cut into bite-size chunks. Arrange on platter. Remove scallions and ginger root. Combine cornstarch with 1/4 cup water and add to liquid in *wok*. Simmer until thickened. Pour over pork.

FRESH HAM—HONG KONG
(Serves 6)

- 1 4-5 lb. fresh ham
- 1 cup water
- 4 green onions, cut into 2-inch lengths
- 1 teaspoon fresh ground ginger
- 2 cups soy sauce
- 1/4 teaspoon anise
- 1/2 cup rice wine *or* sherry
- 1 tablespoon sugar
- 1 clove garlic, crushed
- 6 hard-cooked eggs

Rinse ham in cold water and dry. Bring 1 cup water to a boil and add green onions, ginger, soy sauce, anise, wine, sugar and garlic. Allow to simmer for a few minutes. Add the ham and enough extra water to cover. Bring to a boil, cover and simmer for 3 hours. Remove ham, slice and arrange on a warm platter. Garnish with hard-cooked-egg halves.

HONG KONG SAUCE

- 2 cups ham liquid
- 1 tablespoon cornstarch
- 2 tablespoons water

Skim fat from cooking liquid. Pour two cups of liquid into saucepan and bring to a boil. Combine cornstarch and water. Add cornstarch mixture to liquid. Simmer until thickened. Serve as gravy sauce with ham.

ROUND HAM OF PORK WITH SPINACH
(Serves 6)

2-lb. ham, boned, with skin
3 tablespoons red bean curd
1/4 cup rice wine *or* sherry
1 tablespoon sugar
4 tablespoons soy sauce
1/2 cup hot water
2 tablespoons oil
2 cloves garlic, mashed
2 scallions
Boiling water
2 bunches spinach leaves, separated, washed and drained

Combine red bean curd, wine, sugar, 2 tablespoons soy sauce and 1/2 cup hot water. Scrape surface of skin of meat, and rub with 2 tablespoons of soy sauce. Brown pork in deep pot, skinside down in heated oil. Turn pork over, add garlic cloves, scallions and red-bean-curd mixture. Fry 30 seconds, then add boiling water to cover at least 1 inch over top of pork. Simmer gently for 3 hours or until pork is very tender. Pour 1/2 cup liquid from pork into *wok*, or skillet, and bring to boil. Add spinach leaves. Cover and simmer 2 minutes until leaves are wilted. Drain. Cut pork into 1/4-inch slices. Arrange spinach in a ring on platter. Place pork slices skinside up on spinach.

BASIC STEAMED PORK
(Serves 3 to 4)

1 lb. minced raw pork
1 teaspoon cornstarch
1/2 teaspoon salt
2 teaspoons soy sauce
1/4 teaspoon MSG
Water
1 scallion, chopped—*optional*

Mix all ingredients well and shape into patty on heatproof platter or dish. Place platter on rack in deep pot with 1-1/2 inches water in bottom. Bring water to boil. Cover, reduce heat and steam 30 minutes.

Variations for Steamed Pork

(Follow basic recipe on all following variations.)

SALTED CABBAGE

Add 1/4 cup salted cabbage, soaked to remove excess salt. Chop and mix with pork.

SWEET PICKLED CUCUMBERS

Add 1/4 cup sweet pickled cucumbers, chopped.

WATER CHESTNUTS

Add 1/2 cup chopped water chestnuts.

CHINESE MUSHROOMS

Add 1/2 cup Chinese mushrooms, presoaked and chopped.

CHINESE MUSHROOMS AND WATER CHESTNUTS

Add 1/4 cup Chinese mushrooms, presoaked and chopped, and 1/4 cup water chestnuts, peeled and chopped.

CHINESE MUSHROOMS, WATER CHESTNUTS AND RED DATES

Add 1/4 cup Chinese mushrooms, presoaked and chopped; 1/4 cup water chestnuts, peeled and chopped; and 4 red dates, presoaked 30 minutes, pitted and minced.

CHINESE SAUSAGE

Add 2 or 3 Chinese sausages sliced diagonally 1/8-inch thick and placed on top of patty.

SALTED FISH

Add 1 3-inch square piece salted fish and 1 1/4-inch piece ginger root, slivered or minced, after following basic recipe. In sink, scald fish on both sides with boiling water. Scrape off scales and chop fish into 3 or 4 pieces. Distribute over pork patty and sprinkle with ginger root.

STEAMED PORK CUBES
(Serves 4 to 6)

1 lb. boneless pork, cut into 1-1/2-inch cubes
2 tablespoons soy sauce
1/2 cup rice wine *or* sherry
1/2 cup beef broth
1/4 teaspoon MSG

Mix all ingredients in deep dish or bowl. Place bowl on rack in deep pot with sufficient water to reach base of bowl. Bring water to boil. Reduce heat, cover and steam for 2 hours.

STEAMED PORK WITH SALTED CABBAGE
(Serves 3 to 4)

1 lb. boned pork chops, sliced into thin pieces
1/2 cup finely chopped salted cabbage
2 tablespoons chopped water chestnuts
1 teaspoon peanut oil
1 teaspoon cornstarch
1 teaspoon MSG
2 teaspoons soy sauce

Mix all the ingredients. Arrange on platter and steam on rack in covered *wok*, or skillet, for 30 minutes or until done.

STEAMED MINCED PORK WITH HAM
(Serves 3 to 4)

1 lb. pork, finely chopped
1 cup finely chopped Virginia ham
8 water chestnuts, peeled and chopped
1/4 teaspoon MSG
1 tablespoon soy sauce
1 teaspoon salt
1/2 teaspoon peanut oil
1 teaspoon cornstarch

Mix all ingredients thoroughly. Put in deep platter and shape into patty. In a large pot have 2 inches of boiling water with rack on bottom. Place platter with minced pork-and-ham pancake on rack. Cover and steam 25 minutes or until done.

HOT PORK AND CHICKEN WITH VEGETABLES
(Serves 6 to 8)

1 broiling chicken—approximately 2 lbs.
1 lb. pork
3 tablespoons oil
3/4 cup chopped onion
2 garlic cloves, minced
3 tomatoes, cut into eighths
1 teaspoon salt
1/2 teaspoon dried ground chili pepper
2 tablespoons ground sesame seeds
3/4 cup beef broth
2 tablespoons soy sauce
1 cup cooked or canned green peas

Bone the chicken and dice the meat. Cut the pork in 1-inch cubes. Heat the oil in a *wok*, or skillet, and brown the chicken and pork. Remove to platter. Stir-fry the onion and garlic in the oil remaining in the *wok* until brown. Add tomatoes and cook over low heat 3 minutes. Return the chicken and pork. Add the salt, chili pepper, sesame seeds, broth and soy sauce. Cover and cook over low heat 30 minutes. Add the peas and cook 5 minutes longer or until meat and chicken are tender.

DICED CHICKEN GIBLETS AND PORK
(Serves 4)

1 set chicken giblets (heart, liver, gizzard), cleaned and diced
1 cup diced pork
1 tablespoon peanut oil
1/2 teaspoon salt
1 clove garlic, mashed
1 teaspoon light soy sauce
1 teaspoon minced fresh ginger root
1 teaspoon rice wine *or* sherry
1 cup soup stock
1 tablespoon cornstarch
1/4 teaspoon MSG
1 teaspoon heavy soy sauce
1 teaspoon sugar
1/2 cup water
1/4 cup diced bamboo shoots
1/4 cup diced Chinese black mushrooms
1/4 cup diced celery
1/4 cup diced onion
1/4 cup roasted almonds

Heat peanut oil. Add salt and garlic in *wok*, or skillet. Add chicken giblets and pork. Stir-fry until light brown. Combine light soy sauce, ginger, wine and 1 teaspoon of soup stock. Combine cornstarch, MSG, heavy soy sauce and sugar, and add 1/2 cup water. Add combination to chicken and pork. Then add vegetables. Stir-fry for 2 minutes. Add rest of soup stock, cover and simmer 3 minutes. Stir-fry until gravy thickens. Place in serving bowl and garnish with almonds.

Variation: Add 1/2 cup peas or 1/2 cup sliced cabbage and chives.

PORK CHOP SUEY
(Serves 4 to 6)

1 lb. boneless pork, sliced 2 x 1/2 x 1/8 inches
2 tablespoons oil
1 teaspoon salt
1/4 teaspoon black pepper
1 medium onion, peeled and cut into 6 wedges
2 stalks celery, cut diagonally into 1/4-inch slices
2 tablespoons soy sauce
1 cup beef broth
1 10-oz. can bean sprouts or 1/2 lb. fresh bean sprouts, rinsed and drained
1 tablespoon cornstarch
2 tablespoons water

Mix together the soy sauce, sugar, and broth. Heat oil in *wok*, or skillet, and add salt and pepper. Add the pork and stir-fry until brown. Add sliced onion and celery wedges, and stir-fry. Add beef-broth mixture and bring to a boil. Cover, reduce heat and simmer for 3 minutes. Add bean sprouts. Stir-fry. Cover and simmer another 3 minutes. Combine cornstarch and water, and blend well. Add cornstarch-and-water combination and stir until sauce thickens.

CHINESE BARBECUED PORK
(Serves 4)

2 lbs. boned pork chops or pork shoulder, cut into strips approximately 1-1/2 x 4 inches
1-1/2 teaspoons salt
1 tablespoon sugar
4 tablespoons soy sauce
2 cloves garlic, crushed
2 tablespoons honey
2 tablespoons rice wine *or* sherry
2 tablespoons pineapple juice

Combine soy sauce, garlic, honey, salt, sugar, wine and pineapple juice. Marinate pork in the mixture for 30 minutes. Remove pork and place in broiler or 400° oven for 10 minutes. Lower heat to 250° and roast for 20 minutes (on rack) on each side. Turn off oven, let out some heat, and keep pork in oven until ready to serve.

SWEET-AND-SOUR SPARERIBS
(Serves 4)

1-1/2 lb. spareribs, cut into serving-size pieces, approximately 1-1/2 inches
3 tablespoons soy sauce
1 tablespoon brown sugar
1 teaspoon salt
1 tablespoon cornstarch
1 1/4-inch piece crushed ginger
Fat for frying
3 tablespoons vinegar
1/2 cup water

Marinate ribs in combination of 1 tablespoon soy sauce, brown sugar, salt, cornstarch, and ginger for 10 to 15 minutes. Brown ribs in *wok* in hot fat. Remove excess fat. Add vinegar, water and rest of soy sauce. Bring to boil. Cover, reduce heat and simmer until tender, about 25 to 30 minutes.

PORK SPARERIBS IN BLACK BEAN SAUCE
(Serves 4 to 5)

1-1/2 lbs. pork spareribs
1 1/4-inch fresh ginger root
1 clove garlic, minced
1 heaping tablespoon black beans
2 stalks green onions
1 tablespoon peanut oil
1 teaspoon salt
1/2 cup water *or* soup stock
2 teaspoons soy sauce
1/4 teaspoon MSG
1/2 teaspoon sugar
1 teaspoon cornstarch
3 drops sesame seed oil

Cut ribs into serving-sized strips. Mash ginger and garlic. Wash beans and place in bowl with ginger and garlic. Mash beans with handle of cleaver or large knife. Cut green onions diagonally into 1-1/2-inch pieces. Heat peanut oil in *wok*, or skillet, and add the salt. Sauté ribs in hot oil. Drain excess fat and continue to fry ribs, turning often. Add black-bean mixture, stirring well with ribs. Add water and bring to boiling point. Reduce heat, cover, and cook for 20 minutes. Add soy sauce, MSG, sugar, onions and cornstarch dissolved in water. Mix well. Cook until gravy thickens. Add sesame oil. Mix in thoroughly.

STIR-FRIED PORK WITH ONIONS
(Serves 4)

3/4 lb. pork, tenderloin, boned shoulder or butt, thinly sliced
1 teaspoon rice wine *or* sherry
1 clove garlic, crushed
2 teaspoons soy sauce
1 teaspoon cornstarch
1 teaspoon MSG
1/2 teaspoon sugar
1/4 cup water
Dash pepper
2 tablespoons peanut oil
1/2 teaspoon salt
2 medium onions, thinly sliced
2 scallions—*white part only*—cut into 1-inch lengths
1/2 cup soup stock

Mix together the wine, garlic and 1 teaspoon soy sauce. Combine the other teaspoon soy sauce with cornstarch, MSG, sugar, water and pepper, and stir thoroughly. Heat peanut oil in *wok*, or skillet. Add the salt and pork, and stir-fry until meat is brown. Add wine mixture and stir-fry 1 minute. Add the onions and scallions, and stir-fry 1 minute. Add the soup stock and bring to a boil. Slowly add cornstarch combination, stirring as you pour. Cook until gravy thickens.

PORK WITH VEGETABLES
(Serves 4)

1/2 lb. pork, thinly sliced
1 lb. assorted vegetables such as: celery, green peppers, tomatoes, onions, bean sprouts, asparagus, turnips, carrots, spinach, broccoli, cabbage, Chinese cabbage, mushrooms, bamboo shoots, water chestnuts, scallions, string beans, peas, Chinese pea pods. (Use as many or few as you like, there is no limit or preference.)

Use the same method of cooking and ingredients as in Stir-Fry Pork with Onions, substituting the above vegetables for the onions. Slice and shred the vegetables as you desire.

PORK WITH BAMBOO SHOOTS
(Serves 4 to 5)

1/2 lb. pork, thinly sliced
1 tablespoon soy sauce
1/2 teaspoon salt
2 tablespoons rice wine *or* sherry
1 tablespoon cornstarch
2 tablespoons cooking oil
2 cups sliced bamboo shoots
1/4 cup water

Marinate pork in soy sauce, salt, wine and cornstarch for approximately 15 minutes. Reserve marinade. Heat oil in *wok* and stir-fry pork until light brown. Add bamboo shoots and stir-fry 2 minutes. Add water combined with marinade. Bring to a boil. Cover and simmer for 1 minute, stirring.

PORK WITH FRESH BEAN CURD
(Serves 4)

1/2 lb. pork, cut into thin slices
2 teaspoons soy sauce
1 teaspoon sugar
1 teaspoon rice wine *or* sherry
1/4 teaspoon pepper
1/2 cup water
1 tablespoon cornstarch
1/4 teaspoon MSG
1 tablespoon oyster sauce—*optional*
1 tablespoon peanut oil
1/2 teaspoon salt
1 clove garlic, crushed
4 cakes bean curd, cut into eighths
2 fresh scallions—*white part only*, chopped
1/2 cup thinly sliced onion
4 black mushrooms, presoaked in warm water, sliced

Combine 1 teaspoon soy sauce, sugar, wine and pepper. Combine water, cornstarch, MSG, remaining soy sauce and optional oyster sauce. Heat the peanut oil in *wok*, or skillet, on high flame until it begins to smoke. Add the salt and garlic, and sauté for 10 seconds. Stir-fry the bean-curd squares until slightly brown. Remove and set aside. Then stir-fry the pork until brown and add wine-and-soy sauce mixture. Add the scallions, onion and mushrooms, and cook 5 minutes. Then add the browned bean-curd squares and cook another 5 minutes. Add cornstarch combination and cook until gravy thickens.

BROCCOLI WITH BRAISED PORK
(Serves 4)

1-1/2 lbs. pork, cut into 1-inch cubes
3 tablespoons vegetable oil
1 clove garlic, minced
1 teaspoon minced ginger root *or* 1/2 teaspoon ground ginger
2 tablespoons soy sauce
1 tablespoon rice wine *or* sherry
1 teaspoon sugar
1/4 cup water
1 lb. fresh broccoli, washed and drained, with fibrous outer cover peeled, cut into 2-inch lengths *or* 2 packages of frozen broccoli, thawed and chopped

Heat 2 tablespoons oil in *wok*, or skillet, and add pork. Stir-fry on all sides until brown. Stir in garlic, ginger, soy sauce, wine, sugar and water. Bring to boil, cover, and simmer over low heat 30 minutes. Heat remaining oil in saucepan and cook broccoli over high heat 4 minutes. Drain. Arrange on a serving dish and top with pork.

PORK WITH BROCCOLI AND VERMICELLI
(Serves 4)

1/2 lb. pork-butt, tenderloin or boned shoulder, cut into thin slices
1/4 cup water
1 teaspoon minced fresh ginger root
1 teaspoon rice wine
1/2 teaspoon heavy soy sauce
2 teaspoons light soy sauce
1/4 teaspoon pepper
1/4 teaspoon MSG
1 tablespoon cornstarch
1 tablespoon peanut oil
1 teaspoon salt
6 black mushrooms, presoaked in warm water 1/2 hour, then drained and sliced finely

1/2 lb. broccoli, chopped into 1-inch pieces
1/4 lb. vermicelli, soaked in warm water 30 minutes, then cut into any length desired and drained
1/2 cup soup stock
2 fresh scallions—*white part only*, chopped about 1/2-inch lengths

Combine water, ginger, wine, heavy soy sauce, light soy sauce, salt, pepper, MSG and cornstarch. Heat peanut oil in *wok*, or skillet, until it smokes. Then add pork and stir-fry until golden brown. Add mushrooms and broccoli, and stir-fry 2 minutes. Then add vermicelli and stir-fry another minute. Add soup stock, cover, and simmer over medium heat about 5 minutes. Add cornstarch combination and cook until sauce thickens. Garnish with green onions.

PORK WITH SHREDDED CABBAGE
(Serves 4 to 6)

1 lb. pork
1 teaspoon sugar
1 teaspoon salt
1 tablespoon rice wine *or* sherry
3 tablespoons soy sauce
3 tablespoons oil
1 lb. cabbage, finely shredded
1 garlic clove, minced
1/4 teaspoon pepper

Cut the pork into matchlike pieces and mix with sugar, salt, wine and 2 tablespoons soy sauce. Let stand 10 minutes. Heat 2 tablespoons oil in *wok*, or skillet. Stir-fry the cabbage 1 minute and remove from pan. Heat the remaining oil in the *wok*. Stir-fry the pork and garlic 3 minutes. Add the cabbage, pepper and remaining soy sauce. Cover and cook over low heat 2 minutes.

EGGPLANT AND PORK
(Serves 4 to 6)

1 lb. raw pork
1 clove garlic, minced
1/4 teaspoon cinnamon
2 tablespoons soy sauce
1 teaspoon sugar
1/2 teaspoon salt
2 teaspoons cornstarch
1 teaspoon minced ginger root
3 tablespoons cooking oil
1/2 cup water
1 eggplant, peeled and cubed

Cut the pork into 1/2-inch squares and mix with garlic, cinnamon, soy sauce, sugar, salt, cornstarch and ginger. Allow to marinate 15 minutes. Heat two tablespoons of oil in *wok*, or skillet, and stir-fry the pork for 4 minutes. Add the water. Cover and cook over low heat for 10 minutes. While pork is cooking, heat remaining oil in another skillet and sauté the eggplant for 2 minutes, stirring frequently. Mix the eggplant with the pork. Cover and cook another 5 minutes.

PORK AND GREEN BEANS
(Serves 4)

1/2 lb. pork
1 tablespoon soy sauce
1 teaspoon cornstarch
1 teaspoon sugar
1/2 teaspoon salt
1/4 teaspoon pepper
2 tablespoons oil
1 lb. green beans, cut in halves *or*
    1 package frozen green beans, thawed
1/2 cup boiling water

Cut the pork into bite-size pieces. Mix with soy sauce, cornstarch, sugar, salt and pepper. Let marinate 10 minutes. Heat the oil in *wok*, or saucepan, and stir-fry the pork 5 minutes, stirring frequently. Add the beans and cook 1 minute, stirring constantly. Add the water. Cover and cook over low heat 10 minutes.

GROUND PORK AND GREEN BEANS
(Serves 4)

1/2 lb. ground pork
1 lb. green beans *or* 1 package frozen cut beans, thawed
2 teaspoons cornstarch
1/2 cup water
2 tablespoons oil
3/4 teaspoon salt
1 clove garlic, minced
2 tablespoons soy sauce
1/2 cup sliced water chestnuts
1 cup shredded lettuce
2 green onions, chopped

Wash and cut string beans diagonally into 1/4-inch slices. Mix cornstarch with 1/4 cup water. In *wok*, or skillet, heat the oil, and add salt and garlic. Stir-fry a few seconds. Add the pork and stir-fry till browned. Add soy sauce and water chestnuts, and stir. Add the green beans and 1/4 cup water, and bring to a boil. Cover, reduce heat and simmer 2 minutes. Add above cornstarch mixture slowly, stirring until sauce thickens. Serve in deep bowl on bed of lettuce. Garnish with green onions.

PORK WITH GREEN PEPPERS
(Serves 4 to 6)

3/4 lb. boneless pork, cut into 1/2-inch cubes
2 tablespoons soy sauce
1 teaspoon sugar
1/2 teaspoon minced ginger root
2 tablespoons vegetable oil
1 cup chopped onion
1 cup shredded Chinese cabbage
1 cup Julienne-cut green peppers

Combine soy sauce, sugar and ginger root. Heat the oil in a *wok*, or skillet. Add the pork and onions and stir-fry over medium heat until pork is browned. Add the cabbage, green peppers and soy sauce mixture. Bring to a boil while stir-frying. Reduce heat, cover and simmer 2 minutes.

GREEN PEPPERS STUFFED WITH PORK
(Serves 6 to 8)

3/4 lb. pork, tenderloin or butt
3/4 lb. fresh sole or haddock filet
1 cup fresh or canned crab
1/4 cup black mushrooms, soaked in warm water 15 minutes
1/4 cup water chestnuts, peeled and chopped
1/2 teaspoon MSG
1 teaspoon salt
Dash pepper
2 fresh scallions—*white part only*
8 large green peppers, seeded

Grind all ingredients, except peppers, and mix thoroughly. Stuff peppers and place in colander. Steam 35 minutes in a covered pot with approximately 1-1/2 inches boiling water, or bake in 350° oven for 30 minutes with 1 inch of water in bottom of pan.

PORK WITH LEEKS AND PINEAPPLE
(Serves 4)

1/2 lb. pork, thinly sliced
1 tablespoon soy sauce
1 tablespoon rice wine *or* sherry
1 tablespoon cornstarch
2 tablespoons peanut oil
1 clove garlic, crushed
1 small onion, cut into chunks
2 leeks, split in half lengthwise and cut into 1-inch sections
1 teaspoon minced fresh ginger root
1/2 cup pineapple chunks, drained—*save liquid*

Combine soy sauce, wine and cornstarch, and marinate pork in this mixture for 15 minutes. Drain and save marinade. Heat peanut oil in *wok*, or skillet. Add garlic and stir-fry until browned; then remove and discard. Add pork and stir-fry until browned. Add onion, leeks and ginger, and stir-fry until onion browns. Add the marinade and pineapple juice, and bring to a boil. Add pineapple chunks, blending thoroughly.

PORK WITH CHINESE LONG BEANS AND WATER CHESTNUTS
(Serves 4)

1/2 lb. lean pork, finely minced
10 water chestnuts, peeled and finely diced
1 lb. Chinese long beans, tips trimmed, diced into 1/4-inch pieces
2 stalks celery, cut lengthwise into 1/4-inch strips, and diced into 1/4-inch pieces
1 clove garlic
1/2 cup hot water
1 teaspoon *nam-yu* (Chinese seasoning) *or* 1/2 teaspoon salt
1 tablespoon cornstarch
1 tablespoon soy sauce
1 tablespoon water
1/4 cup blanched toasted almonds, chopped

Sauté pork in hot greased *wok*, or skillet, for 5 minutes. Add vegetables and stir-fry, mixing ingredients well. Add hot water and *nam-yu*, or salt, and cook 3 minutes. Add soy sauce, cornstarch and 1 tablespoon water mixture, and cook 2 more minutes, or until gravy thickens. Add almonds.

PORK WITH PEAPODS AND TURNIPS
(Serves 4)

1/2 lb. pork
1 teaspoon rice wine *or* sherry
2 teaspoons soy sauce
1 teaspoon sugar
1 tablespoon peanut oil
1 teaspoon salt
1 clove garlic, crushed
1 cup peapods, break off tips and remove "string"
1 cup Chinese turnips
1/2 medium onion, sliced
1/4 cup black or white mushrooms, presoaked and sliced
1/4 cup canned bamboo shoots, sliced into thin strips
1/2 cup soup stock
1/2 cup water
1 tablespoon cornstarch
1 teaspoon MSG

Combine wine, soy sauce and sugar. Heat peanut oil in *wok*, or skillet, until it smokes. Add the salt and garlic, and stir-fry 5 seconds. Remove garlic (if desired) and add pork. Stir-fry until brown. Add the wine mixture and stir for a few seconds. Add the peapods, Chinese turnips, onion, mushrooms, bamboo shoots, MSG, and soup stock. Simmer, covered, 3 minutes. Mix water with cornstarch. Add cornstarch mixture and cook until gravy thickens.

BRAISED PORK AND SPINACH
(Serves 4 to 6)

1 5-rib pork loin, boned—approximately 2-1/2 lbs.
1 clove garlic, minced
1 teaspoon salt
1/4 teaspoon black pepper
2 tablespoons honey
1/4 cup soy sauce
1 cup beef broth *or* water

2 tablespoons rice wine *or* sherry
2 teaspoons cornstarch
3 tablespoons oil
2 bunches fresh spinach, washed and trimmed *or* 2 packages frozen leaf spinach, thawed

Rub the pork with garlic, salt and pepper. Combine the honey, soy sauce, 3/4 cups broth and wine. Combine the cornstarch with 1/4 cup broth. Heat the oil in *wok*, or skillet, and brown the pork on all sides. Pour off all but 2 tablespoons of fat. Pour the honey mixture over pork and bring to simmer. Cover and cook over low heat 1 hour or until tender. Baste and turn meat frequently. Remove the meat. Stir-fry spinach in 1 tablespoon oil for a few seconds, and cover; simmer for 2 minutes. Arrange the spinach in the center of serving dish. Cut the pork into slices and place on top of bed of spinach. Thicken sauce in *wok* with cornstarch mixture, and pour over pork.

BRAISED PORK WITH SPINACH
(Serves 6 to 8)

3 lbs. pork loin
4 tablespoons soy sauce
1-1/2 tablespoons brown sugar
1 cup hot beef broth or hot water
2 lbs. spinach, washed and trimmed *or* 2 packages frozen spinach, thawed

Brown the pork in *wok*, or heavy saucepan. Pour off most of the fat. Add the soy sauce, brown sugar and broth or water. Cover and cook over low heat until very tender. Remove meat and keep warm. Cook spinach in the sauce remaining in the pan for 3 minutes. Place on a platter. Slice pork and arrange on top of spinach.

PORK AND WATER CHESTNUTS
(Serves 2 to 4)

1/2 lb. pork
8 water chestnuts, peeled
1 tablespoon cornstarch
1 tablespoon water
1 head lettuce
2 tablespoons peanut oil
1/2 teaspoon salt
1 teaspoon soy sauce
Dash black pepper
1/4 cup chicken broth

Mince together pork and water chestnuts. Combine cornstarch and water. Separate lettuce leaves, wash and drain and arrange on plate. Heat peanut oil in *wok*, or skillet, and add pork and water chestnuts, salt, soy sauce and pepper. Stir-fry 1 minute. Add chicken broth. Cover and simmer 2 minutes. Add cornstarch mixture gradually and stir-fry until thickened. Serve alongside bowl containing lettuce leaves. Diner wraps spoonful of misture in individual lettuce leaf and eats with fingers.

STIR-FRIED PORK WITH BAMBOO SHOOTS
(Serves 4)

1 lb. boneless pork, diced
1 tablespoon rice wine *or* sherry
3 tablespoons soy sauce
2 tablespoons cornstarch
1/4 cup peanut oil
1/4 cup sliced green onion
1 cup diced bamboo shoots
2 teaspoons sugar

Marinate pork in wine, sugar, and soy sauce. Roll the diced pork in the cornstarch. Heat peanut oil in *wok*, or skillet, and add the pork and green onion. Stir-fry until pork is browned. Add the bamboo shoots, sugar and remaining soy sauce. Stir and simmer for 5 minutes.

STIR-FRIED PORK WITH GREEN ONIONS
(Serves 4)

1 lb. boneless pork, cut into 1/8 x 1/2 x 2-inch slices
1/4 cup soy sauce
1 tablespoon rice wine *or* sherry
5 tablespoons vegetable oil
1 1/4-inch slice ginger root, minced
2 bunches green onions, cut into 2-inch lengths
1 teaspoon salt

In bowl, mix pork with soy sauce and wine. Heat the oil in a *wok*, or skillet. Add ginger root, then pork, and stir-fry until pork loses its pink color. Add the green onions and salt, and stir-fry over high heat for 30 seconds.

STIR-FRIED PORK WITH PEAPODS
(Serves 4)

1/2 lb. pork, thinly sliced
2 tablespoons soy sauce
1 teaspoon sugar
1 teaspoon rice wine *or* sherry
1/2 cup water
1 tablespoon cornstarch
1/4 teaspoon MSG
Dash pepper
1 lb. peapods, ends and strings removed
1 tablespoon peanut oil
1 teaspoon salt
1 clove garlic, crushed
1/2 cup soup stock

Mix together 1 tablespoon soy sauce, sugar, wine and 1 tablespoon of water. Combine the remaining water, cornstarch, 1 tablespoon soy sauce, MSG and pepper. Bring peapods to a quick boil and drain. Heat peanut oil in *wok*, or skillet, over high flame until smoking hot. Add salt and garlic, and sauté 10 seconds. Add the pork and stir-fry quickly until pork browns. Add wine mixture and stir. Add the peapods and soup stock. Cover and cook 3 minutes. Add cornstarch combination and stir-fry until gravy thickens.

STIR-FRIED SWEET-AND-SOUR PORK IN EGG BATTER
(Serves 4)

1 lb. boneless pork shoulder, cut into 1-inch cubes
1/2 cup cider vinegar
1/4 cup brown sugar
1 tablespoon molasses
1-1/4 cups water
1 egg, beaten
1/2 teaspoon salt
1/2 cup flour
2 tablespoons peanut oil
1 tablespoon cornstarch
1 8-oz. can pineapple wedges
1 tomato, cut into 6 wedges

Combine vinegar, brown sugar, molasses and 3/4 cup water. Mix beaten egg with salt, flour and 1/4 cup of water until it becomes a smooth batter. Dip pork cubes into batter. Coat well on all sides. Heat peanut oil in *wok*, or skillet, and fry batter-coated pork until browned on all sides. Drain and keep hot. Pour vinegar combination into *wok* and bring to boiling point. Add cornstarch and remaining water, and stir until thickened. Add the pineapple and tomato wedges, and simmer 3 to 5 minutes. Add hot pork.

PORK CHOPS CATHAY
(Serves 4 to 6)

6 pork chops
2 tablespoons peanut oil
Salt *to taste*
Pepper *to taste*
1/2 cup flour
1 clove garlic, minced
1/2 teaspoon crushed dried chili pepper
1/2 cup soy sauce
1/2 cup rice wine *or* sherry
2 teaspoons sugar
3 stalks green onion, chopped
1/4 teaspoon sesame oil
1/2 teaspoon MSG
1 teaspoon toasted sesame seed

Heat peanut oil in *wok*, or skillet. Salt and pepper pork chops, coat with flour and brown in oil. Combine remaining ingredients, except toasted sesame seeds, and pour mixture over chops. Cook, covered, 30 to 40 minutes or until chops are tender. Baste and turn occasionally. Place chops on platter and garnish with toasted sesame seeds.

PORK CHOPS WITH OYSTER SAUCE
(Serves 2)

1 lb. boned pork chops, approximately 4
2 cloves garlic, crushed
4 tablespoons oyster sauce
Dash pepper

Sprinkle garlic over meat and broil or fry. Brush with oyster sauce and pepper.

DEEP-FRIED PORK WITH MIXED VEGETABLES
(Serves 4 to 6)

1 lb. pork, diced into 1-inch squares
2 tablespoons soy sauce
Dash pepper
1 teaspoon sugar
1 teaspoon rice wine *or* sherry
1 tablespoon water
1/4 cup water
1/4 teaspoon MSG
1 tablespoon cornstarch
1 teaspoon heavy soy sauce
2 eggs, beaten
3/4 cup flour
1/2 teaspoon salt
1 cup peapods, stringed, washed and drained
1 cup thinly sliced Chinese cabbage
1 medium onion, sliced
4 water chestnuts, peeled and sliced
1/4 cup bamboo shoots, sliced into 2-inch lengths
1 tablespoon peanut oil
Oil for frying
1 clove garlic
1/4 cup soup stock

Combine soy sauce, pepper, sugar, wine and 1 tablespoon water. Combine 1/4 cup water, MSG, cornstarch and heavy soy sauce. Combine eggs, flour and salt. Combine peapods, cabbage, onion, water chestnuts and bamboo shoots. Marinate pork in wine mixture for 10 minutes. Then mix with egg combination. Deep fry coated pork cubes in oil until golden brown. Heat oil in *wok*, or skillet, and stir-fry garlic until brown. Then discard or use as desired. Add combined vegetables and stir-fry for 2 minutes. Then add deep-fried pork and mix well. Add soup stock. Cover and simmer for 2 minutes. Slowly add the combination of water and cornstarch, and cook until gravy thickens.

DEEP-FRIED PORK BALLS WITH LETTUCE
(Serves 3 to 4)

1 lb. raw pork, tenderloin or butt, finely chopped
1 cup finely chopped fresh lean Virginia ham
3 scallions, finely chopped
1 cup black mushrooms, soaked in warm water 15 minutes and finely chopped
1/4 cup peeled water chestnuts, finely chopped
1/4 teaspoon MSG
1 teaspoon soy sauce
1-1/2 teaspoons sugar
1/2 teaspoon salt
1/2 teaspoon pepper
1/2 teaspoon curry powder
1 teaspoon rice wine *or* sherry
1/2 cup cornstarch
2 eggs, beaten
1 quart peanut oil
1 head lettuce
Catsup
Hot mustard

To the pork, ham, scallions, mushrooms and water chestnuts, add the MSG, soy sauce, sugar, salt, pepper, curry powder, and wine. Mix well. Add the cornstarch and eggs and stir until mixture has a pastelike quality. Roll into balls about 1 inch in diameter. Pour the peanut oil into a *wok*, or skillet, and heat to smoking point. Pick up balls, one by one, and fry until golden brown. Serve with lettuce leaves and mixture of hot mustard and catsup (to taste).

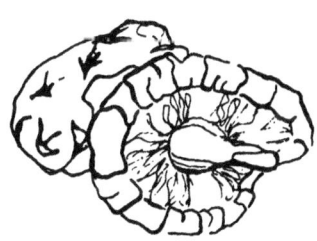

SPICY TWICE-COOKED SZECHWAN PORK
(Serves 4)

3/4 lb. lean pork
1 scallion, slivered lengthwise and cut into 1-inch lengths
2 tablespoons *hoy sin* sauce
1 teaspoon sugar
1/2 teaspoon crushed red pepper
3/4 cup chicken broth *or* pork liquid
1 tablespoon cornstarch
2 tablespoons oil
1 1/4-inch slice ginger root, minced
1 clove garlic, minced
1 cup bean sprouts

In saucepan, cover pork with cold water. Bring to boil, then cover and simmer 20 minutes. Remove meat and allow to cool. Slice into 1/4-inch-thick pieces. Combine scallion, *hoy sin* sauce, sugar, and pepper with 1/4 cup broth. Combine cornstarch with 1/2 cup broth. In hot *wok*, or skillet, add oil and heat until just smoking. Add ginger and garlic. Stir-fry few seconds, then add pork. Stir-fry until pork pieces are browned. Add *hoy sin* mixture. Bring to boil, then simmer 1 minute. Stir in bean sprouts, cover and simmer 3 minutes. Add cornstarch mixture. Stir-fry until sauce thickens.

chicken

A chicken in every pot! I vaguely recall that to have been someone's campaign slogan. But the importance of chicken is not necessarily limited to the political scene. I prefer to see it featured on the dining room table. Chicken is perhaps the most economical of meats. I suggest you buy your birds whole, rather than cut up. They are much less expensive if purchased that way. It is also much more practical to purchase whole chickens because the meat can be boned and used for your new or favorite Chinese dishes, and the gizzards, bones and neck used as the base for a perfect broth you can use in your cooking or as a soup stock.

In many of the chicken dishes that follow, duck or pork can be substituted, or pork and chicken can be used in combination.

CHICKEN WITH ALMONDS AND MUSHROOMS
(Serves 4 to 6)

2 chicken breasts, boned and diced
3 tablespoons oil
1 teaspoon salt
1/4 teaspoon pepper
2 tablespoons soy sauce
1/2 cup diced celery
1/2 cup peas, fresh or frozen
1/4 cup diced onion
1 4-oz. can button mushrooms, drained
1 cup hot chicken broth
1 teaspoon cornstarch
2 tablespoons water
1/2 cup blanched almonds, toasted

Heat the oil in a *wok*, or skillet, and stir-fry the chicken for 3 minutes. Add salt, pepper, soy sauce, celery, peas, onion and mushrooms. Cook for 2 minutes, then stir in broth. Cover and cook over low heat for 5 minutes. Mix together the water and cornstarch, and stir into mixture until it thickens. Add the almonds and serve.

CHICKEN WITH ALMONDS AND WATER CHESTNUTS
(Serves 4 to 6)

1 lb. raw chicken, boned and sliced
2 tablespoons oil
1/4 cup split almonds
1 teaspoon salt
1/4 teaspoon pepper
1/2 cup fresh sliced mushrooms
1/2 cup sliced water chestnuts
2 tablespoons soy sauce
3 tablespoons water
1 tablespoon cornstarch

In *wok*, or skillet, heat oil and add chicken, almonds, salt, pepper, and stir-fry until chicken is browned. Add mushrooms, water chestnuts, soy sauce and 1 tablespoon water, and stir-fry. Cover, lower heat and simmer 3 minutes. Combine cornstarch and remaining 2 tablespoons water, and add to chicken mixture. Cook and stir until sauce thickens.

CHICKEN AND BELL PEPPERS
(Serves 4 to 6)

2 chicken breasts, skinned and boned
3 tablespoons oil
2 tablespoons soy sauce
1/2 teaspoon salt
1/4 teaspoon pepper
1 teaspoon cornstarch
1 clove garlic, minced
2 bell peppers
2 celery stalks, diced diagonally into 1/4-inch pieces
1 small onion, chopped
2 scallions, split lengthwise, then cut into 2-inch pieces
1/4 teaspoon sugar
1/4 cup cold water

Cut the chicken into small squares and marinate with mixture of 1 tablespoon oil, 1 tablespoon soy sauce, salt, pepper, cornstarch and garlic. Let stand for 20 minutes. Cut peppers and remove seeds. Cut into 1-inch squares. Heat the remaining oil in *wok*, or skillet, and stir-fry the peppers, celery and onions for 2 minutes. Add the scallions, and sauté another 1 minute. Remove the vegetables. Add the chicken to the *wok* and stir-fry for 3 minutes. Mix the remaining cornstarch and soy sauce, sugar and water. Add to the chicken mixture in *wok*, and cook until sauce thickens. Arrange chicken and vegetables on platter.

CHICKEN AND BLACK MUSHROOMS
(Serves 6)

    1 4-lb. roasting chicken, quartered
    1 tablespoon cornstarch
    1/4 teaspoon sugar
    1/4 cup water
    4 tablespoons soy sauce
    3 tablespoon rice wine *or* sherry
    1 teaspoon salt
    1/2 teaspoon pepper
    2 teaspoons minced ginger root
    1 clove garlic, minced
    2 tablespoons oil
    8 dried Chinese mushrooms, soaked in water 30 minutes, drained and sliced
    3/4 cup chicken broth

Combine cornstarch, sugar, water and 1 tablespoon soy sauce. Wash and dry the chicken. Mix together 3 tablespoons soy sauce, wine, salt, pepper, ginger and garlic. Rub into chicken and let stand 30 minutes. Heat the oil in *wok*, or skillet, and brown the chicken well. Add the mushrooms and broth. Cook, covered, over low heat for 30 minutes. Remove chicken, cut into small pieces and arrange on platter. Add cornstarch combination and bring to simmer. Cook until sauce thickens. Pour over chicken.

CHICKEN WITH BUTTON MUSHROOMS
(Serves 3 to 4)

    2 chicken breasts, skinned, boned and cut into 1/4 x 2-inch strips
    2 teaspoons cornstarch
    1 tablespoon soy sauce
    1/8 teaspoon pepper
    3 tablespoons oil
    1 4-oz. can button mushrooms
    1 teaspoon salt
    1 clove garlic, minced
    1 teaspoon minced ginger root

Combine 1 teaspoon cornstarch, soy sauce, pepper and 1 tablespoon oil, and marinate the chicken mixture for 20 minutes. Drain the mushrooms, reserving 1/4 cup of the liquid. Mix the remaining cornstarch with the mushroom liquid and add salt. Heat the remaining oil in a *wok*, or skillet, and add the chicken, garlic and ginger. Stir-fry for 2 minutes. *Don't* allow it to brown. Add the mushrooms and stir-fry another 1 minute. Add the cornstarch marinade and stir until it thickens. Cover and simmer another 1 minute.

CHICKEN WITH CHESTNUTS
(Serves 4)

- 1 3-lb. chicken
- 1 teaspoon salt
- 1/4 teaspoon pepper
- 2 tablespoons soy sauce
- 2 tablespoons rice wine *or* sherry
- 1 lb. chestnuts, unshelled
- 2 tablespoons oil
- 6 scallions, splintered lengthwise and cut into 1-1/2 to 1-inch pieces
- 1 teaspoon minced ginger
- 1 cup chicken broth
- 1 tablespoon cornstarch—*optional*
- 2 tablespoons water—*optional*

Cut the chicken into small pieces; quarter the breasts. In bowl, mix the salt, pepper, soy sauce and wine thoroughly. Marinate chicken pieces for 20 minutes. Cut a cross on the top of each chestnut. Cover with water in saucepan and bring to a boil. Cook over medium heat for 15 minutes. Drain and shell. Heat oil in *wok*, or skillet, and brown the chicken. Add the scallions, ginger and then the broth. Cook, covered, over low heat for 20 minutes. Add chestnuts and cook 15 minutes longer. Thicken sauce with mixture of 1 tablespoon cornstarch and two tablespoons water (optional).

CHICKEN WITH HAM AND BROCCOLI
(Serves 6)

1 3-lb. chicken
1 medium onion
1 tablespoon salt
6 cups water
1 tablespoon cornstarch
1/4 teaspoon MSG
12 slices ham
1 bunch broccoli, stems separated, blanched and drained

Place chicken, onion, salt and water in deep saucepan, and bring to a boil. Lower heat, cover and simmer for 30 minutes. Cool, then slice the chicken. Boil broccoli 3 minutes in broth. Strain and measure out 1 cup of the broth. Mix the cornstarch with a little broth and the MSG, then stir into broth. Cook over low heat until thickened. Taste for seasoning. Arrange alternate slices of ham and chicken on a dish with broccoli. Pour sauce over all.

CHICKEN WITH PINEAPPLE
(Serves 4)

1 lb. chicken, cut into 1-inch cubes
1 tablespoon cornstarch
1/2 teaspoon salt
2 teaspoons cold water
1 teaspoon soy sauce
1 teaspoon MSG
3 tablespoons peanut oil
1/2 cup onion, sliced
1/2 cup celery, cut diagonally
1/2 cup pineapple chunks
4 tablespoons pineapple juice
1 tablespoon sugar
1 tablespoon rice wine *or* sherry

Combine cornstarch, salt, cold water, soy sauce and MSG. Marinate chicken in this mixture for 1/2 hour. In *wok*, or skillet, heat 1 tablespoon of peanut oil and add the onion and celery. Stir-fry for 2 minutes and remove. Heat the remaining 2 tablespoons peanut oil in *wok* and stir-fry the chicken until browned. Return the celery and onions to the *wok* and add all the remaining ingredients. Stir-fry the whole mixture and simmer for 1 minute.

CHICKEN AND TOMATOES
(Serves 4)

2 chicken breasts, skinned, boned and cut into squares
2 tablespoons soy sauce
1 tablespoon rice wine *or* sherry
2 tablespoons cornstarch
2 tablespoons oil
1 cup onion, 1-inch chunks
1 teaspoon salt
1 teaspoon sugar
1/2 cup chicken broth
2 medium tomatoes, cut into eighths

Combine 1 tablespoon soy sauce, wine and 1 tablespoon cornstarch, and marinate chicken in the mixture for 20 minutes. Heat the oil in *wok*, or skillet, and sauté the chicken for 3 minutes. Stir in onions and sauté another 2 minutes. Mix the remaining soy sauce, cornstarch, salt, sugar and broth. Add to the *wok* and stir until thickened. Stir in tomatoes and cook until heated.

CHICKEN AND WALNUTS
(Serves 4)

2 chicken breasts, boned
2 tablespoons soy sauce
2 tablespoons rice wine *or* sherry
1 teaspoon sugar
2 tablespoons cornstarch
1/2 teaspoon minced fresh ginger root
Oil for deep frying
1/2 cup walnuts
3 tablespoons oil
1/4 cup cubed or sliced bamboo shoots
1/4 cup sliced celery
4 water chestnuts, peeled and sliced
1/4 cup chicken stock

Combine soy sauce, wine, sugar, 1 tablespoon cornstarch and ginger. Marinate chicken in this mixture for 1 hour. Deep fry chicken in *wok*, or skillet. Drain and cut into pieces. Boil walnuts for 3 minutes; drain well. Then deep fry until slightly brown. Heat 2 tablespoons oil in *wok*, or skillet, until smoking and add all the vegetables. Stir-fry for 2 minutes. Add the chicken and walnuts, and fry another 1 minute. Combine soup stock with remaining 1 tablespoon cornstarch, and add to mixture. Cook until the sauce thickens.

CHICKEN WITH CASHEWS

Same ingredients and cooking method as above, substituting 1/2 cup cashews for walnuts.

CHICKEN WITH ALMONDS

Same ingredients and cooking method as above, substituting 1/2 cup blanched, roasted almonds for walnuts.

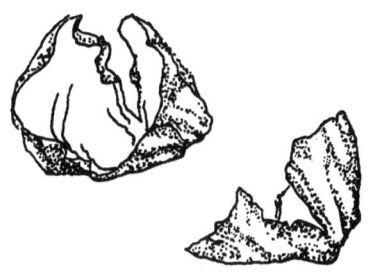

SPICY SZECHWAN CHICKEN WITH TANGERINE PEEL
(Serves 4)

1 lb. chicken breast, fileted or sliced
2 tablespoons dried tangerine peel pieces, presoaked
Oil for deep frying
1 tablespoon *hoy sin* sauce
1/2 teaspoon crushed red pepper
1/2 cup chicken broth
1/2 teaspoon sugar
1 tablespoon cornstarch
2 tablespoons oil
1 teaspoon minced fresh ginger root
1 clove garlic, minced
2 scallions, cut into 2-inch lengths

Soak pieces of tangerine in cold water for 1 hour. Drain and save liquid. Blot pieces dry in paper toweling. Deep fry pieces of tangerine peel in oil. When crisp, remove from oil and let drain on paper towel. Set aside. Combine *hoy sin* sauce, pepper, chicken broth, and sugar. Separately, combine cornstarch with 2 tablespoons soaking liquid from tangerine peel. In *wok*, or skillet, heat 2 tablespoons oil. Add ginger and garlic, and stir-fry a few seconds. Add scallions. Then add chicken and stir-fry until slightly brown. Add *hoy sin* sauce mixture and bring to a boil. Cover and simmer 3 minutes. Add cornstarch mixture, and stir until sauce is thickened. Stir in crisp pieces of tangerine peel. Serve hot or cold.

FRIED CHICKEN—CHINESE STYLE
(Serves 3 to 4)

1 4-6 lb. chicken, cleaned and dried
1/2 cup soy sauce
1 tablespoon brown bean sauce
1 teaspoon sugar
1 teaspoon rice wine *or* sherry
1 teaspoon minced fresh ginger
1 clove garlic, crushed
Dash pepper
1 teaspoon salt
Peanut oil for deep frying

Combine soy sauce, bean sauce, sugar, wine, ginger, garlic, pepper and salt. Cut chicken in 1/2 and marinate in this mixture for 1 hour or more. Steam marinated chicken in double boiler for about 30 minutes. Cool. Deep fry chicken in peanut oil until golden brown. Cut each 1/2 into 3 pieces.

CANTONESE FRIED CHICKEN
(Serves 4 to 6)

1 3-lb. chicken, cut up
2 tablespoons soy sauce
3 tablespoons rice wine *or* sherry
1 clove garlic, minced
1 teaspoon sugar
1/2 cup cornstarch
Fat for frying

Wash and dry the chicken. Make sure chicken breasts are quartered. Rub with soy sauce, wine, garlic and sugar combined, and let stand for 15 minutes. Then coat chicken with the cornstarch. Heat the fat in a *wok*, or skillet, and fry the chicken until golden brown. Drain off some of the fat. Cook, covered, over low heat for approximately 15 minutes.

FRIED BONELESS CHICKEN CANTONESE
(Serves 3 to 4)

1 4-6 lb. chicken
1/2 cup soy sauce
1 tablespoon brown bean sauce
1 teaspoon sugar
1 teaspoon rice wine *or* sherry
1 teaspoon minced fresh ginger
1 clove garlic, crushed
Dash pepper
1 teaspoon salt
2 eggs, well beaten
3/4 cup cornstarch
Pinch MSG
Pinch salt
Oil for deep frying

Combine soy sauce, brown bean sauce, sugar, wine, ginger, garlic, pepper and salt. Cut chicken in 1/2 and marinate in this mixture for 1 hour or more. Combine into a batter-type mixture the eggs, cornstarch, MSG and pinch of salt. Steam marinated chicken in double boiler about 30 minutes. Remove bones. Roll pieces of chicken in batter mixture. Heat deep oil in *wok*, or skillet. Add chicken and deep fry until golden brown.

STIR-FRIED CURLED CHICKEN WITH VEGETABLES
(Serves 4 to 6)

1 lb. chicken white meat, thinly sliced and cut into 3-inch squares
2 teaspoons soy sauce
1 teaspoon rice wine *or* sherry
1 teaspoon minced fresh ginger root
1 tablespoon water
1 tablespoon cornstarch
1/4 teaspoon MSG
1 teaspoon sugar
Dash pepper
1/2 cup water
1 tablespoon peanut oil
1 teaspoon salt
1 clove garlic, mashed
1 cup peapods, ends trimmed and cut in 1/2 crosswise
1/4 cup thinly sliced bamboo shoots
1 cup Chinese cabbage, sliced about the size of the peapods
1/2 cup thinly sliced celery
1/4 cup canned or fresh water chestnuts, peeled and thinly sliced
1/2 onion, sliced
1 green scallion, cut in 1/2 and then into 1-inch pieces
1 cup soup stock.

Combine 1 teaspoon soy sauce, wine, ginger and 1 tablespoon water. Stir well. Combine rest of soy sauce, cornstarch, MSG, sugar, pepper and 1/2 cup water. Stir well. Heat peanut oil in *wok*, or skillet, and add salt and garlic. Add the chicken meat and stir-fry until meat curls. Then add wine mixture and stir-fry 1 minute. Add peapods, bamboo shoots, Chinese cabbage, celery, water chestnuts and onions. Stir-fry 2 minutes. Then add scallions and soup stock. Cover and cook 3 minutes. Add cornstarch combination and cook until gravy thickens and is smooth.

STIR-FRIED CURLED CHICKEN WITH LICHEE
(Serves 3 to 4)

1 lb. chicken white meat, thinly sliced and cut into 3-inch squares
2 teaspoons soy sauce
1 teaspoon rice wine *or* sherry
1 teaspoon minced fresh ginger
1 tablespoon water
1 teaspoon cornstarch
1 teaspoon MSG
1 teaspoon sugar
Dash pepper
1/2 cup water
1 tablespoon peanut oil
1 teaspoon salt
1 clove garlic, mashed
1/4 cup thinly sliced bamboo shoots
1/4 cup canned or fresh water chestnuts, peeled and thinly sliced
1/2 cup onion
1 green scallion, cut in 1/2 and then into 1-inch pieces
1 cup soup stock
1 cup canned lichee

Combine light soy sauce, wine, ginger and 1 tablespoon water. Stir well. Combine heavy soy sauce, cornstarch, MSG, sugar, pepper and 1/2 cup water. Stir well. Heat peanut oil in *wok*, or skillet, and add salt and garlic. Add chicken meat and stir-fry until meat curls. Add wine mixture and stir-fry 1 minute. Add bamboo shoots, celery, water chestnuts and onion. Stir-fry for 2 minutes. Then add scallions, soup stock and lichee. Cover and cook 3 minutes. Then add cornstarch combination, stirring until sauce thickens.

DEEP-FRIED CHICKEN IN BATTER WITH VEGETABLES
(Serves 6)

1 lb. chicken meat, cut into 1-inch cubes
2 teaspoons rice wine *or* sherry
1 teaspoon sugar
1/2 teaspoon minced fresh ginger
3-4 drops sesame seed oil
3 teaspoons soy sauce
2 eggs, beaten
3/4 cup flour
Pinch of salt
1/2 teaspoon MSG
1 teaspoon heavy soy sauce
1 tablespoon cornstarch
Dash pepper
1/4 cup water
Oil for deep frying
1 tablespoon peanut oil
1/2 teaspoon salt
1 clove garlic, mashed
1 cup fresh Chinese peapods
1/2 cup sliced bamboo shoots
2 water chestnuts, peeled and sliced
1/4 cup black mushrooms, presoaked 20 minutes and sliced

Combine wine, sugar, ginger, sesame seed oil and 2 teaspoons soy sauce. Combine the beaten eggs, flour, pinch of salt and the MSG, and beat into smooth batter. Combine 1 teaspoon soy sauce, cornstarch, dash of pepper and 1/4 cup water. Marinate chicken meat in 1/2 of the wine mixture for 30 minutes. Heat enough oil for deep frying in *wok*, or skillet. Dip chicken pieces in egg batter, and deep fry until golden brown. Drain and put aside. Heat peanut oil in *wok*. Add salt and garlic and stir-fry a few seconds. Add the peapods, bamboo shoots, cabbage, water chestnuts and mushrooms and stir-fry for 2 minutes. Add second half wine mixture and stir thoroughly. Add soup stock, cover, and simmer for 3 minutes. Add cornstarch combination, and stir-fry until sauce thickens. Place cooked vegetables in deep serving dish and top with fried chicken pieces.

CHICKEN POT ROAST
(Serves 6)

1 3-lb. frying chicken—rinse and chop liver and gizzard
2 teaspoons cornstarch
1-1/4 cups water *or* mushroom soaking liquid
1 teaspoon minced ginger root
1 clove garlic, minced
1 tablespoon rice wine *or* sherry
2 tablespoons soy sauce
8 dried Chinese mushrooms, soaked in warm water 30 minutes—*save liquid*
2 tablespoons oil
6 scallions, split lengthwise then cut into 2-inch pieces
1 teaspoon salt
1/4 teaspoon pepper
1/2 teaspoon sugar

Combine cornstarch and 1/4 cup water. Wash and dry chicken. Combine the ginger, garlic, wine and soy sauce, and rub mixture well inside and outside the chicken. Let stand about 30 minutes. Drain the mushrooms and slice. In deep pot, heat the oil and brown the chicken on all sides. Remove from pot. Add the gizzards, mushrooms and scallions, and stir-fry for 1 minute. Then add the remaining water, salt, pepper and sugar. Bring to boil. Return the chicken. Cover and let simmer 45 minutes. Remove chicken, cool and chop into small pieces. Add cornstarch mixture to liquid in pot. Bring to simmer and cook until sauce thickens. Pour over chicken.

SPICED ROAST CHICKEN
(Serves 4)

1 4-lb. roasting chicken
1/4 cup soy sauce
2 cloves garlic, minced
2 teaspoons salt
1/4 teaspoon pepper
1 teaspoon sugar
1 teaspoon five-spice mixture
2 tablespoons oil
Lettuce leaves

Wash and dry chicken. Mix together soy sauce, garlic, salt, pepper, sugar, five-spice mixture and oil. Thoroughly rub inside and outside of the chicken with mixture. Let it stand for 1 hour. Place the chicken on rack in roasting pan and roast for 2 hours at 425°. Baste and turn the chicken often. Cut the chicken into sections or small pieces and arrange on bed of shredded lettuce.

CHICKEN ROASTED WITH TANGERINE PEEL
(Serves 4)

1 4-6 lb. chicken, cleaned and dried
1/2 teaspoon MSG
3 teaspoons soy sauce
1 teaspoon dried tangerine peel, presoaked 30 minutes, drained and minced
1 tablespoon rice wine *or* sherry
1 teaspoon brown bean sauce
2 cups chicken soup stock
Light soy sauce

Combine MSG, soy sauce, tangerine peel, rice wine and soup stock. Tie chicken's neck with string. Rub this mixture inside chicken and truss. Brush skin with light soy sauce and place on flat roasting pan. Roast in preheated 450° oven for 10 minutes. Reduce heat to 300° and roast 25 minutes longer. Chop into small pieces or carve.

SWEET-AND-SOUR CHICKEN
(Serves 4)

1 lb. chicken, cut into 1-inch cubes
1 teaspoon MSG
1 teaspoon soy sauce
1/4 teaspoon salt
1/2 cup flour
2 eggs, well beaten
1 tablespoon cornstarch
1/2 cup water
Oil for deep frying
1/2 cup vinegar
1/2 cup sugar
1 cup sweet pickles, cut into 1/4-inch slices

Combine MSG, soy sauce and salt to form marinade. Blend flour and eggs into smooth batter. Marinate chicken for 15 minutes. Remove chicken from marinade and dip into batter mixture, coating it well on all sides. Mix cornstarch with 1/4 cup water. Deep fry chicken in *wok*, or skillet, until golden brown. Drain and set aside. Drain oil from *wok*. Add vinegar and 1/4 cup water. Then add sugar and simmer until it dissolves. Return the chicken to the mixture and add the pickles. Then add cornstarch mixture and stir-fry until sauce thickens.

Note: You may substitute 1-1/2 cups sliced celery, onion chunks and bell pepers for sweet pickles.

CURRIED CHICKEN
(Serves 2 to 3)

1 1-lb. boned chicken, cut into small pieces approximately 1/2-inch square
1 tablespoon oyster sauce
2 tablespoons curry powder
1 teaspoon rice wine *or* sherry
1 teaspoon minced fresh ginger
1 tablespoon water
1 teaspoon sugar
1 tablespoon cornstarch
2 teaspoons soy sauce
1/2 teaspoon MSG
4 tablespoons water
2 tablespoons peanut oil
1 teaspoon salt
2 cloves garlic, mashed
1 cup soup stock
1 green scallion, split and cut into 1-inch lengths

Combine oyster sauce, curry powder, wine, ginger and 1 tablespoon of water. Stir well. Combine sugar, cornstarch, heavy soy sauce, MSG and 4 tablespoons water. Stir well. Heat peanut oil in *wok*, or skillet, and add salt and garlic. Sauté. Then add chicken pieces and stir-fry until golden brown. Add wine mixture and stir-fry for 1 minute. Then add soup stock. Cover and simmer until tender. (Add more soup stock if necessary.) Add cornstarch combination and stir-fry until sauce thickens and is smooth. Garnish with green onions.

Note: You may add chopped onions, sliced celery, bell pepper chunks or potato chunks with chicken.

SOY CHICKEN
(Serves 3 to 4)

1 3-4 lb. whole chicken
1/2 cup soy sauce
1/2 cup water
3 tablespoons brown sugar
1 small piece anise seed
1 1/4-inch slice ginger, crushed
1 tablespoon rice wine *or* sherry
2 teaspoons thick red Chinese soy sauce—*optional*
1 bunch Chinese parsley

Combine and mix thoroughly all ingredients, except chicken and Chinese parsley. Marinate chicken in mixture for 1 hour. Place chicken and marinade in deep saucepan and bring liquid to boil. Then simmer, covered, for 25 to 30 minutes or until tender. Turn chicken over once so that it browns evenly. Chop into serving pieces and arrange on platter. Top with Chinese parsley.

STEAMED SOY SAUCE CHICKEN
(Serves 3 to 4)

1 3-4 lb. whole chicken, cleaned and dried
1 quart soy sauce
1 teaspoon crushed ginger root
1 tablespoon sugar
1/4 cup rice wine *or* sherry
1 tablespoon peanut oil
1 teaspoon sesame seed oil

Marinate chicken in soy sauce, ginger, sugar and wine overnight. Brush chicken thoroughly with peanut oil and sesame seed oil. Place chicken on rack in pot and steam for 25 minutes or until tender. Chop into serving pieces.

CHICKEN PUFFS
(Serves 4)

2 chicken breasts, skinned and boned
1/4 cup water
1 teaspoon cornstarch
5 egg whites
1-1/2 teaspoons salt
1/8 teaspoon pepper
1/4 teaspoon MSG
Oil for deep frying
Puff Sauce
2 tablespoons minced ham

Chop the chicken breasts very fine and add 1 tablespoon water to keep them moist. Mix in the cornstarch, 1 egg white, salt, pepper, MSG and remaining water. Beat the remaining egg whites until stiff and fold into chicken mixture. Heat the oil to 365° and drop chicken mixture into it, one teaspoonful at a time. Fry until browned. Drain on paper towels. Prepare Puff Sauce. Add the chicken puffs and cook 2 minutes. Taste for seasoning. Place on platter. Garnish with minced ham.

PUFF SAUCE

1 tablespoon cornstarch
3/4 cup chicken broth
1 tablespoon rice wine *or* sherry

Mix the cornstarch with a little broth to make a paste; then blend into remaining broth and wine. Cook in saucepan over low heat, stirring, until thickened.

CHINESE CHICKEN SALAD—NUMBER ONE
(Serves 4 to 6)

2 chicken breasts
1 small head lettuce
3 stalks green onion
1 cucumber
2 tablespoons sesame oil
1/4 cup pineapple juice
Salt *to taste*
Pepper *to taste*
2 tablespoons soy sauce
1 tablespoon sugar
2 tablespoons rice wine *or* sherry
2 tablespoons pineapple juice
1/4 teaspoon MSG
Oil for deep frying
1/2 cup pineapple chunks—*save liquid*
1 cup deep-fried noodles *or* long rice
1 tablespoon toasted sesame seeds

Cut lettuce, green onions and cucumber in strips about 2 inches long. Combine sesame oil, 1/4 cup pineapple juice and season to taste. Combine soy sauce, sugar, wine, 2 tablespoons pineapple juice and MSG, and marinate chicken in combination for 1 hour. Heat oil in *wok*, or skillet, and deep fry chicken. Cool, bone, and shred into fine strips. Combine vegetables, sesame oil combination, pineapple chunks, noodles and chicken. Toss and sprinkle with sesame seeds.

CHINESE CHICKEN SALAD—NUMBER TWO
(Serves 4 to 6)

2 chicken breasts
1/2 cup soy sauce
2 tablespoons sugar
3 tablespoons rice wine *or* sherry
1/4 teaspoon MSG
2 stalks green onion
8 Chinese pickled scallions
1 tablespoon toasted sesame seeds
Sesame seed oil
1 teaspoon dry mustard
Salt *to taste*
Pepper *to taste*
1 teaspoon *hoi sin* sauce
1/2 package won ton skin—more, if desired

Combine soy sauce, sugar, wine and MSG, and marinate chicken in mixture for 1 hour. Save marinade mixture. Roast chicken until tender. Cool, bone, and shred meat into 1-inch pieces. Slice green onions lengthwise, then cut into 2-inch pieces. Slice pickled scallions into thin slivers. Combine chicken, green onion, sesame seeds and add approximately 1 teaspoon sesame seed oil. Add the mustard and salt and pepper to taste. Add *hoi sin* sauce and a little marinade sauce. Mix well and let stand until ready to serve. Slice won ton noodles into very thin strips and deep fry. Add crisp fried won ton noodles to chicken mixture and toss lightly just before serving.

beef

China has not been famous for its cowboys or cattle ranches, and beef dishes have never been an important or truly authentic part of the Chinese cuisine. Most Chinese concentrated on pork or poultry.

However, the Chinese pioneers who came to these shores didn't find an abundance of hogs here in the West because these domesticated animals were difficult to raise in an unsettled and constantly moving society. Cattle, being much easier to feed and requiring little care, became the favored livestock. With native ingenuity and ability, the Chinese chefs readily adapted Chinese cooking methods and recipes to include beef dishes.

Beef has a distinct flavor that can be, but generally is not, mingled with pork or chicken. Flank steak is generally preferred for Chinese dishes because of its flavor, texture and easy adaptability for preparation. When slicing beef, pieces should be cut across the grain. This breaks the fibers and permits marinating liquids to penetrate the meat more readily. This slicing technique also makes the bite-size pieces more tender when cooked.

BROILED GINGER STEAK
(Serves 4 to 6)

2 lbs. sirloin or spencer steak
1 cup soy sauce
2 tablespoons minced Chinese ginger root
2 scallions—*white portion only*, minced
2 cloves garlic, minced
1/2 cup sugar
1/2 cup rice wine *or* sherry
1 teaspoon MSG
1 teaspoon salt

Combine all ingredients in bowl and marinate meat for 2 hours. Drain meat and broil over smoldering charcoal or in broiler as desired.

BRAISED BEEF CHUNKS
(Serves 4 to 6)

1-1/2 lbs. chuck beef, cut in 1-1/2-inch chunks
2 tablespoons oil
1 teaspoon minced ginger root
1 clove garlic, minced
2 tablespoons soy sauce
1 tablespoon rice wine *or* sherry
2 points star anise
1/4 teaspoon salt
1 teaspoon oyster sauce
Several drops sesame oil
1-1/2 cups hot water
1 teaspoon cornstarch
2 tablespoons cold water

In *wok*, or skillet, heat oil and brown beef chunks on all sides. Add remaining ingredients, except hot water and cornstarch, and stir-fry 1 minute. Add hot water. Cover and simmer 45 minutes or to desired tenderness. Make paste of cornstarch and cold water, and stir into mixture until sauce thickens.

BEEF BALLS ROASTED IN WINE SAUCE
(Serves 4 to 6)

    1 lb. lean ground beef
    1 teaspoon cornstarch
    2 teaspoons sugar
    2 teaspoons rice wine *or* sherry
    1/2 teaspoon ginger powder
    1 teaspoon oyster sauce
    Few drops sesame oil
    1/4 cup plus 2 teaspoons soy sauce
    1 clove garlic, minced
    1/4 cup water

Blend beef with cornstarch, 1 teaspoon sugar, 1 teaspoon wine, 1/4 teaspoon ginger powder, oyster sauce and sesame oil, and roll into 1-inch-diameter balls. Arrange in flat roasting pan. Combine balance of sugar, wine, soy sauce, garlic and water, and pour over beef balls. Place beef balls in 275° oven. Cook, uncovered, 45 minutes. Baste occasionally with liquid in pan.

Note: May be served as appetizer on cocktail picks.

BASIC STEAMED SLICED BEEF
(Serves 4 to 6)

1 lb. sirloin or flank steak
1 tablespoon cornstarch
1 tablespoon rice wine *or* sherry
2 tablespoons soy sauce
1 tablespoon sugar
1/4 teaspoon MSG
1 teaspoon salt
1 teaspoon oyster sauce—*optional*
3-4 drops sesame oil
Chinese parsley or green onion, chopped

Slice beef with grain into 2-inch-wide strips, then slice across grain into slices 1/8-inch thick. In bowl, combine remaining ingredients into smooth mixture and blend well with beef slices. Then spread thinly on platter or in shallow bowl. Spread 1 of following ingredients evenly over meat spread:

1/4 cup pickled bamboo shoots, rinsed and drained
8 dried Chinese mushrooms, presoaked 1 hour, drained and thinly sliced
1/2 cup dates, pitted and coarsely chopped
1/4 cup salted cabbage, soaked, squeezed dry and chopped
3 tablespoons sweet preserved cucumbers with 1 tablespoon pickled bamboo shoots, chopped
1/4 cup cloud's ear fungus, soaked and drained and 1 square-inch piece of tangerine peel, soaked and minced

Place platter of beef spread on rack in *wok*, skillet or deep pot, with adequate water for steaming. Bring water to boil. Cover and steam 8 to 10 minutes. Stir once so all meat is cooked evenly. Garnish with green onion or parsley.

STEAMED BEEF BALLS
(Serves 4 to 6)

1 lb. lean ground beef
1 1/4-inch slice ginger root, minced
1 small onion, finely chopped
1 tablespoon soy sauce
1 tablespoon cornstarch
1 teaspoon rice wine *or* sherry
1 teaspoon oyster sauce
1/2 teaspoon sugar
1/4 teaspoon salt
Several drops sesame oil

In deep bowl, blend together all ingredients. Roll mixture into balls 1-inch in diameter and arrange on heat-proof platter or plate. Place meat on rack in *wok*, or pot. Cover and steam 15 to 20 minutes.

STEAMED BEEF WITH WATER CHESTNUTS
(Serves 4 to 6)

1 lb. lean ground beef
6 water chestnuts, peeled and minced
3 dried Chinese mushrooms, presoaked, drained and chopped
1 tablespoon cornstarch
1 tablespoon rice wine *or* sherry
2 teaspoons soy sauce
1 teaspoon sugar
1 teaspoon oyster sauce
1/4 teaspoon sesame oil
Chopped green onions or Chinese parsley

Mix all ingredients, except green onions or parsley, in bowl. Remove mixture from bowl and form into flat pancake or patty on heat-proof plate. Place plate on rack in deep pot or pan with enough water not to boil over top of rack. Bring water to boil. Reduce heat, cover, and steam 6 to 8 minutes. Remove and garnish with green onions or Chinese parsley.

BEEF WITH ASPARAGUS
(Serves 4 to 6)

1/2 lb. flank steak
2 teaspoons soy sauce
1/2 teaspoon sugar
1 tablespoon cornstarch
2 teaspoons rice wine *or* sherry
1/4 cup water
1/4 teaspoon MSG
3 tablespoons oil
1/4 teaspoon salt
1 clove garlic, crushed
1 1/4-inch piece ginger root, minced
1 lb. asparagus, tender parts of stems diagonally cut in 1/4-inch slices, leave tips whole
1/4 cup soup stock *or* water
1 green onion cut into 2-inch slivers
Black bean sauce—*optional*

Cut steak *with* grain 2 inches, then *across* grain into strips 1/8 inch thick. Combine soy sauce, sugar, cornstarch, wine, water and MSG, and set aside. Heat 2 tablespoons oil in *wok*, or skillet. Add salt, garlic and ginger, and stir-fry a few seconds. Add beef and stir-fry until barely pink. Remove and set aside. Heat remaining oil in *wok* and add asparagus. Stir-fry a few seconds and add soup stock. Cover and simmer 4 minutes. Add cornstarch mixture and stir until sauce thickens. Garnish with green onions.

BLACK BEAN SAUCE

1 tablespoon black beans, soaked in water a few minutes and drained
1 clove garlic
1 1/4-inch slice ginger root

Mince and crush together the black beans, garlic and ginger root. Stir-fry sauce mixture a few seconds in *wok* just before adding asparagus, if desired.

BEEF WITH FRESH BEAN CURD
(Serves 4 to 6)

1/2 lb. flank steak
3 teaspoons cornstarch
2 teaspoons soy sauce
2 teaspoons sugar
1 teaspoon rice wine *or* sherry
2 tablespoons water
3 tablespoons oil
1 clove garlic, crushed
1 tablespoon brown bean sauce
2 cakes fresh bean curd, cubed
2 stalks green onion, chopped

Cut steak lengthwise in 2-inch strips, then across grain into 1/8-inch slices. Marinate beef in mixture of 1 teaspoon cornstarch, soy sauce, 1 teaspoon sugar and wine for 20 minutes. Combine remaining 2 teaspoons cornstarch into a paste with the water. In *wok*, or skillet, heat 2 tablespoons oil. Then add garlic and beef and stir-fry quickly for 1 minute. Remove beef and set aside. Add remaining tablespoon of oil and heat. Then add brown bean sauce and 1 teaspoon sugar, and stir-fry. Mix ingredients well. Add bean curd, cover and simmer 3 minutes. Return beef and stir-fry. Then add cornstarch mixture and cook until sauce thickens. Garnish with green onion.

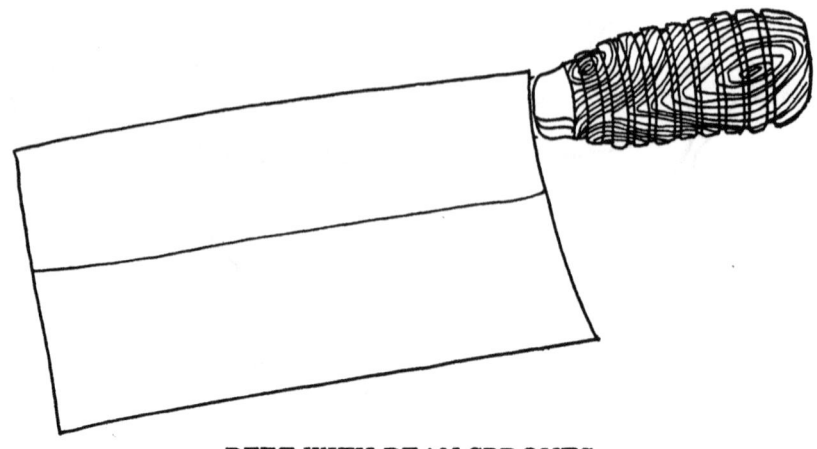

BEEF WITH BEAN SPROUTS
(Serves 4 to 6)

1/2 lb. flank or sirloin steak
2 teaspoons soy sauce
1 teaspoon sugar
2 teaspoons rice wine *or* sherry
1 teaspoon cornstarch
4 tablespoons water
4 tablespoons oil
1 teaspoon salt
1 teaspoon minced ginger root
1/4 cup diagonally sliced celery
1/4 cup sliced onion
1/4 cup sliced bamboo shoots
1/2 lb. bean sprouts, washed and drained

Cut steak into 2-inch-wide pieces, then across grain into 1/8-inch slices. In bowl, marinate beef 30 minutes in mixture of soy sauce, sugar and wine. Combine cornstarch with 2 tablespoons water. In *wok*, or skillet, heat 2 tablespoons oil. Add 1/2 teaspoon salt and ginger, and stir-fry a few seconds. Add the beef and fry until just pink. Remove and set aside. Heat remaining oil in *wok* and add celery, onion, bamboo shoots and remaining 1/2 teaspoon salt. Stir-fry. Cover and simmer 1 minute. Add bean sprouts and simmer another minute. Return beef and mix with vegetables. Add cornstarch mixture and stir until sauce thickens.

BEEF WITH BELL PEPPERS
(Serves 4)

1/2 lb. sirloin or flank steak
2 teaspoons soy sauce
1 teaspoon sugar
1 teaspoon rice wine *or* sherry
1 teaspoon oyster sauce
1 tablespoon cornstarch
1/4 cup water
3 tablespoons oil
1 teaspoon salt
1 1/4-inch slice of ginger root, minced
2 bell peppers, seeds removed
1 onion, peeled and cut into eighths
1 tablespoon water
1 green onion, chopped

Cut steak into 2-inch pieces lengthwise and into 1/8-inch slices across the grain. Marinate beef in mixture of soy sauce, sugar, wine, oyster sauce for 20 minutes. Combine cornstarch with 1/4 cup water. In *wok*, or skillet, heat 2 tablespoons oil. Add salt and ginger and stir-fry a few seconds. Add beef and stir-fry very short time leaving the meat still pink. Remove and set aside. Heat the remaining tablespoon of oil. Rinse bell peppers, cut them into 1-1/2-inch squares, and add. Separate onion into layers and add. Stir-fry. Add 1 tablespoon water. Cover and simmer 1 minute. Return beef and stir. Then add cornstarch mixture and stir slowly until sauce thickens. Serve garnished with green onion.

BEEF WITH TOMATOES
(Serves 4)

Follow recipe and directions for Beef with Bell Peppers, eliminating bell peppers and substituting:

2 medium tomatoes, cut into eighths
1 stalk celery, sliced diagonally into 1/8-inch slices

Note: Bell peppers and tomatoes can be combined using one or more of each.

BEEF WITH GREEN PEAS, ONIONS AND MUSHROOMS
(Serves 4)

Follow recipe and directions for Beef with Bell Peppers, eliminating bell peppers and substituting:

> 1 package frozen green peas and small onions, thawed
> 4 Chinese mushrooms, presoaked in warm water, drained and finely sliced—substitute soaking liquid for water in recipe

BEEF WITH FRESH MUSHROOMS
(Serves 4)

Follow recipe and directions for Beef with Bell Peppers, eliminating bell peppers and substituting 8 medium mushrooms. Wash the mushrooms and slice with stems intact.

BEEF WITH BITTER MELON
(Serves 4 to 6)

> 1/2 lb. flank steak
> 1 lb. bitter melon, halved lengthwise
> 2 teaspoons soy sauce
> 1 teaspoon sugar
> 1 teaspoon rice wine *or* sherry
> 1 tablespoon cornstarch
> 1/4 cup water
> 3 tablespoons oil
> 1 teaspoon salt
> 1 1/4-inch slice fresh ginger root, minced
> 1 clove garlic, minced
> 2 tablespoons water

Cut steak across grain into 2 x 1/2 x 1/4-inch strips. Remove fibers and seeds from melon, then cut crosswise into 1/4-inch slices. Blanche and drain bitter melon. Marinate beef in mixture of soy sauce, sugar and wine for 20 minutes. Combine cornstarch with 1/4 cup water. In *wok*, or skillet, heat 2 tablespoons oil and add 1/2 teaspoon salt, ginger, and garlic. Slightly brown meat, remove and set aside. Heat remaining 1 tablespoon of oil in *wok* and add bitter melon. Stir-fry a few seconds and add 2 tablespoons water. Cover and simmer 4 minutes. Return the beef to *wok* and cornstarch mixture. Stir until sauce thickens.

BEEF AND BITTER MELON WITH BLACK BEAN SAUCE
(Serves 4 to 6)

Follow recipe and directions for Beef with Bitter Melon, adding:

1 tablespoon black beans

Mince and mash together garlic and black beans, instead of stir-frying garlic with beef. Stir-fry garlic-and-black bean mixture with bitter melon recipe before adding water and simmering.

BEEF WITH BROCCOLI
(Serves 4 to 6)

1/2 lb. sirloin or flank steak
2 teaspoons cornstarch
1 tablespoon soy sauce
2 teaspoons rice wine *or* sherry
2 teaspoons sugar
3 tablespoons water
3 tablespoons oil
1 teaspoon salt
1 lb. broccoli

Cut steak into pieces 2 inches wide, then across grain into 1/4-inch slices. Marinate beef in mixture of 1 teaspoon cornstarch, soy sauce, wine and 1 teaspoon sugar for 30 minutes. Strip fibrous outside from stems of broccoli and cut into small pieces. Combine remaining cornstarch with 1 tablespoon water. In *wok*, or skillet, heat 2 tablespoons oil and add 1/2 teaspoon salt. Add beef and stir-fry until slightly pink. Remove and set aside. Heat remaining oil and add 1/4 teaspoon salt. Then add broccoli. Stir-fry 1 minute, then add 2 tablespoons water. Cover and simmer 5 minutes or until stems are tender. Return beef and mix. Add cornstarch mixture and cook until sauce thickens.

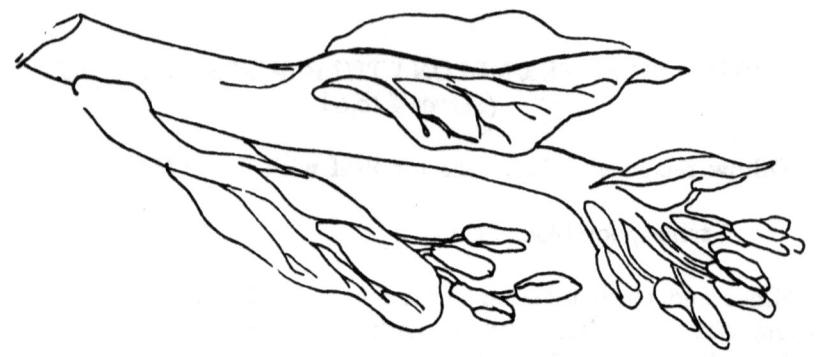

BEEF WITH CHINESE BROCCOLI
(Serves 4 to 6)

1/2 lb. beef strips, 2 x 1/8 x 1/2 inches
1 lb. Chinese broccoli
1 tablespoon soy sauce
2 teaspoons sugar
3 teaspoons rice wine *or* sherry
1 teaspoon cornstarch
3 tablespoons water
3 tablespoons cooking oil
1 teaspoon salt
1 1/4-inch slice fresh ginger, minced

Coarsely cut leaves of Chinese broccoli and tender upper portion of stems into 2-inch lengths. Strip off fibrous outside of base of stems and cut into small pieces. In bowl, marinate beef in mixture of soy sauce, 1 teaspoon sugar and 2 teaspoons wine, for 30 minutes. Combine cornstarch, remaining teaspoon of sugar and wine with 1 tablespoon water. Set aside. In *wok*, or skillet, heat 2 tablespoons oil and add 1/2 teaspoon salt and ginger, and stir-fry a few seconds. Add beef and fry until still barely pink. Remove and set aside. Heat remaining oil and add broccoli. Stir-fry and add remaining 2 tablespoons water. Bring to simmer, cover and cook 3 minutes. Return beef. Stir-fry to mix and add mixture of cornstarch. Cook until sauce thickens.

BEEF WITH CAULIFLOWER
(Serves 4 to 6)

1/2 lb. beef strips, 1/8 inches thick by 2 inches long and 1/2 inch wide
2 teaspoons cornstarch
1 tablespoon soy sauce
1 teaspoon sugar
2 teaspoons rice wine *or* sherry
1 tablespoon black beans, presoaked 15 minutes and drained
1 large clove garlic, minced
1 1/4-inch slice ginger root, minced
1-1/2 cups bite-size cauliflower sections
1-1/2 teaspoons salt
1 large clove garlic, mashed
2 teaspoons water
3 tablespoons oil

Marinate beef in mixture of 1 teaspoon cornstarch, soy sauce, sugar and wine for 30 minutes. Mash and mix together the black beans, minced garlic and ginger root. Parboil cauliflower until almost tender with 1 teaspoon salt and mashed garlic clove added to water. Drain and remove garlic. Combine 1 teaspoon cornstarch with 2 teaspoons water. In *wok*, or skillet, heat 2 tablespoons oil. Stir-fry beef until still slightly pink. Remove and set aside. Heat remaining oil in *wok* and add 1/2 teaspoon salt; then add black bean mixture and stir-fry 10 seconds. Add cauliflower and mix, stir-frying. Cover and lower flame. Simmer 5 minutes. Test for desired tenderness with fork. Return beef and mix. Add cornstarch mixture and cook until sauce thickens.

BEEF WITH CHINESE CHARD
(Serves 4 to 6)

1/2 lb. sirloin or flank steak
2 teaspoons soy sauce
1 teaspoon sugar
2 teaspoons rice wine *or* sherry
1 teaspoon cornstarch
2 tablespoons water
3 tablespoons oil
1 teaspoon salt
1 1/4-inch slice fresh ginger root, minced
1/2 lb. Chinese chard

Combine soy sauce, sugar and wine. Combine cornstarch and water into smooth paste. In *wok*, or skillet, heat 2 tablespoons oil. Add 1/2 teaspoon salt and ginger. Stir-fry a few seconds. Add beef and stir-fry until slightly pink. Add soy sauce mixture and fry a few seconds. Remove beef and liquid, and set aside. Cut white portions of chard into 2-inch lengths, or diagonally 1/4-inch wide. Shred leafy portion very coarsely. Heat remaining oil in *wok* and add remaining salt and white part of chard. Stir-fry and cover 10 seconds. Uncover and add green leafy parts and mix. Cover and cook 1 minute. Return beef to *wok* and mix with vegetables. Add cornstarch mixture and stir until sauce thickens.

BEEF WITH CHINESE LONG BEANS
(Serves 4 to 6)

1/2 lb. flank or sirloin steak
2 teaspoons soy sauce
1 teaspoon sugar
2 teaspoons rice wine *or* sherry
1 teaspoon cornstarch
4 tablespoons water
1 teaspoon oyster sauce—*optional*
Few drops sesame oil—*optional*
3 tablespoons oil
1 teaspoon salt
1 1/4-inch slice ginger root, minced
1/2 medium onion, peeled and sliced
1 lb. Chinese long beans, washed and drained

Cut steak *with* grain into 2-inch-wide pieces, then *across* grain into 1/8-inch slices. In bowl combine soy sauce, sugar, wine and cornstarch. Add beef and marinate 30 minutes. Combine cornstarch with 2 tablespoons water, oyster sauce and sesame oil and set aside. In *wok*, or skillet, heat 2 tablespoons oil. Add 1/2 teaspoon salt and ginger, and stir-fry a few seconds. Add beef and onion, and fry until barely pink. Remove and set aside. Remove long bean tips and cut beans into 2-inch lengths. Heat the remaining tablespoon oil and add long beans. Stir-fry a few seconds and add the remaining 2 tablespoons water. Cover and simmer 3 minutes. Return beef and stir-fry. Add soy sauce mixture and stir until sauce thickens.

BEEF WITH STRING BEANS
(Serves 4 to 6)

Same directions as recipe for Beef with Chinese Long Beans using 1/2 lb. string beans instead. Simmer string beans 5 minutes.

BEEF WITH FRENCH-CUT STRING BEANS
(Serves 4 to 6)

Same directions as recipe for Beef with Chinese Long Beans, using 1/2 lb. french-cut string beans instead. Simmer 2 to 3 minutes.

BEEF AND SNOW PEAS
(Serves 4 to 6)

1/2 lb. flank steak
2 teaspoons soy sauce
3 teaspoons cornstarch
1 teaspoon sugar
2 teaspoons rice wine *or* sherry
Dash pepper
1/4 cup soup stock
3 tablespoons oil
1/2 teaspoon salt
1 1/4-inch slice fresh ginger root, minced
1-1/2 cup snow peas, stringed and washed

Cut steak into 2-inch wide strips and then 1/4-inch thick pieces. Combine 1 teaspoon soy sauce, 1 teaspoon cornstarch, 1/2 teaspoon sugar and the wine, and mix with beef. Mix remaining cornstarch, sugar, soy sauce and pepper with soup stock. In *wok*, or skillet, heat 2 tablespoons oil. Add salt and ginger, and stir-fry a few seconds. Add beef and stir-fry until brown. Remove and set aside. Heat remaining oil in *wok* and add snow peas. Stir-fry 1/2 minute. Add beef and fry, mixing for 1/2 minute. Add second cornstarch mixture and stir occasionally until sauce thickens.

BEEF WITH CHINESE TURNIPS
(Serves 4 to 6)

1/2 lb. flank steak
1 lb. Chinese turnips
2 teaspoons soy sauce
1 teaspoon sugar

Beef

1 teaspoon rice wine *or* sherry
1 tablespoon cornstarch
4 tablespoons water
4 tablespoons oil
1 teaspoon salt
1 1/4-inch slice ginger root, minced
1 clove garlic, minced
1 green onion, chopped

Quarter turnips lengthwise, then cut crosswise into 1/4-inch slices. Parboil until almost tender, and drain. Cut steak into 2-inch pieces, then cut across grain into 1/8-inch slices. Combine soy sauce, sugar and wine, and marinate beef in mixture for 30 minutes. Combine cornstarch and two tablespoons water and set aside. In *wok*, or skillet, heat 2 tablespoons oil and slightly brown beef. Remove and set aside. Heat remaining 2 tablespoons oil in *wok*, 1/2 teaspoon salt, ginger and the garlic, and stir-fry a few seconds. Add Chinese turnips and stir-fry another minute. Return beef to *wok* and stir-fry. Add cornstarch mixture and cook slowly until sauce thickens. Garnish with green onion.

Note: For variety, use same recipe as above substituting any of the following vegetables for the Chinese turnips:

1 lb. rutabagas

1 lb. parsnips—omit garlic

1 lb. celery root

1 lb. zucchini—trim off ends, quarter lengthwise and cut into 2-inch lengths.

1 lb. Chinese okra—peel off ridges, wash and cut into 1/4-inch slices

1 lb. Chinese cabbage—leaves washed and cut into 1-1/2-inch-square pieces

1 lb. cabbage—same as Chinese cabbage

3/4 lb. lotus root—cut into 1/2 lengthwise, then sliced crosswise into 1/8-inch slices, adding 1/2 onion, sliced and 1 stalk celery, sliced diagonally

1 lb. summer squash—trim off tops and cut out bottoms; then cut into bite-size wedges

1 lb. mustard greens—wash leaves and cut into 1-1/2-inch squares—omit garlic

2 bunches spinach—washed and very coarsely shredded, drained—add 1 teaspoon oyster sauce to beef marinade

STIR-FRIED BEEF WITH MUSHROOMS AND BAMBOO SHOOTS
(Serves 4 to 6)

1/2 lb. flank steak
2 teaspoons soy sauce
2 teaspoons rice wine *or* sherry
1 teaspoon sugar
1 1/4-inch slice fresh ginger root, minced
1 teaspoon cornstarch
1 tablespoon water
3 tablespoons oil
1 teaspoon salt
1/2 cup sliced fresh mushrooms
1/2 cup sliced bamboo shoots
1/4 cup water

Cut steak 2-inches wide *with* grain and sliced *across* grain into 1/8-inch thick slices. Combine soy sauce, wine, sugar and ginger root. Combine cornstarch and 1 tablespoon water, and mix into paste. In *wok*, or skillet, heat 2 tablespoons oil and add 1/2 teaspoon salt. Then add meat and stir-fry until slightly brown. Add soy sauce mixture and simmer a few seconds. Remove meat and set aside. Heat remaining oil in *wok*. Add mushrooms and bamboo shoots. Stir-fry 2 minutes. Add 1/4 cup water. Cover and simmer 2 minutes. Return meat and fry a few seconds. Cover and simmer 2 minutes. Stir constarch mixture into *wok* and cook until sauce thickens.

BEEF CHOP SUEY
(Serves 4 to 6)

3/4 lb. beef stew meat
1 tablespoon cornstarch
1/4 cup water
2 tablespoons peanut oil
1 teaspoon salt
1/4 teaspoon black pepper
1 medium onion, cut into 6 wedges
4 stalks celery, diagonally cut into 1/4-inch slices
1 teaspoon molasses
1 tablespoon soy sauce
1/4 cup hot beef broth
1 10-oz. can bean sprouts *or* 1/2 lb. fresh bean sprouts

Combine cornstarch and water. Blend well. Heat peanut oil in *wok*, or skillet, and add salt and pepper. Add beef and stir-fry until brown. Add onion wedges and celery pieces, and stir-fry over low heat for 2 minutes. Add molasses, soy sauce and beef broth. Cover and simmer over low heat for 10 minutes. Then add bean sprouts. Cover and simmer another 2 minutes. Add cornstarch mixture and cook until sauce thickens.

BEEF IN GRAVY SAUCE
(Serves 4 to 6)

1 lb. sirloin or flank steak, cut in chunks
2 tablespoons oil
1 teaspoon sugar
4 teaspoons soy sauce
1 tablespoon cornstarch
1/2 cup water
1/4 teaspoon MSG
1/2 teaspoon salt
1 clove garlic, minced

Marinate beef in 1 tablespoon oil, 1 teaspoon sugar and 2 teaspoons soy sauce for 15 to 20 minutes. Combine remaining sugar, soy sauce, cornstarch, the water and MSG. Heat remaining oil in *wok*, or skillet, and add salt and garlic. Stir-fry until garlic is slightly brown. Add beef and stir-fry until barely pink. Add cornstarch mixture and cook until gravy thickens.

BEEF WITH CURRY
(Serves 4)

1 lb. sirloin or flank steak
2 teaspoons soy sauce
1 teaspoon oyster sauce
1 teaspoon sugar
1 teaspoon rice wine *or* sherry
2 teaspoons cornstarch
1/4 cup soup stock *or* water
2 tablespoons oil
1/2 teaspoon salt
1 1/2-inch slice ginger root, minced
2 tablespoons curry powder
1 large onion, peeled, halved and sliced
1 green onion, chopped

Cut steak lengthwise into 2-inch pieces, then across grain into 1/8-inch slices. Marinate beef for 20 minutes in mixture of soy sauce, oyster sauce, sugar, wine and 1 teaspoon cornstarch. Combine remaining teaspoon cornstarch with soup stock. In *wok*, or skillet, heat oil. Add salt and ginger, and stir-fry a few seconds. Add curry powder and onions. Mix and fry a few more seconds. Add beef and fry until beef is barely pink. Add soup stock mixture. Bring to simmer and stir-fry until sauce thickens. Garnish with green onions.

BEEF WITH GINGER
(Serves 4 to 6)

1 lb. sirloin or flank steak, sliced 1/4 x 1/2 x 2 inches
2 teaspoons soy sauce
2 teaspoons rice wine *or* sherry
1 teaspoon sugar
1 teaspoon cornstarch
1/4 cup water
1/4 teaspoon MSG
2 tablespoons oil
1 teaspoon salt
1/4 cup very thin fresh ginger root slices
1/4 cup green onion, white part cut into 1-inch lengths

Combine soy sauce, wine and sugar. Combine cornstarch, water and MSG. Heat oil in *wok*, or skillet, and add salt. Add beef, ginger root and green onions (white part), and stir-fry 1 minute. Add soy sauce mixture and fry until beef is barely pink. Add cornstarch mixture and cook until gravy thickens.

BEEF WITH OYSTER SAUCE
(Serves 4 to 6)

1 lb. sirloin or flank steak, sliced 1/4 x 1/2 x 2 inches
2 teaspoons soy sauce
2 teaspoons rice wine *or* sherry
1 teaspoon sugar
1 teaspoon cornstarch
2 tablespoons water
1/2 teaspoon salt
2 tablespoons oil
1/3 cup scallions—*white part only*, cut into 1-inch lengths
3 tablespoons oyster sauce

Marinate beef in mixture of soy sauce, wine and sugar for 20 minutes. Combine cornstarch and water. Heat oil in *wok*, or skillet, and add salt. Stir-fry 2 seconds, and add beef and scallions. Stir-fry until meat is barely pink. Add oyster sauce and fry another minute. Add cornstarch mixture and cook until gravy thickens.

BOILED BEEF TONGUE
(Serves 6 to 8)

1 beef tongue, 2-1/2 to 3 lbs.
1 1-inch piece ginger root, crushed
2 cloves garlic, crushed
4 whole anise seeds
3/4 cup soy sauce
1/2 cup sugar
1/4 cup rice wine *or* sherry

Place beef tongue in deep pot. Cover with cold water and cook until a few seconds after water reaches boiling point. Pour off water. Place all other ingredients in pot with beef tongue. Add water to barely cover and bring to boil. Reduce heat and simmer 1-1/2 to 2 hours or until tender. Remove skin and return to boiling liquid in pot for 5 minutes. Remove and slice.

STIR-FRIED CALF LIVER
(Serves 4 to 6)

3/4 lb. calf liver, cut and sliced into small strips
2 tablespoons soy sauce
2 teaspoons rice wine *or* sherry
1 teaspoon oyster sauce
Several drops sesame oil
3 tablespoons oil
1/2 teaspoon salt
3 stalks green onion (white part), cut in 2-inch lengths and slivered

Combine soy sauce, wine, oyster sauce and sesame oil. In *wok*, or skillet, heat oil and add salt and green onions. Stir-fry a few seconds. Add liver and stir-fry quickly till liver is lightly browned. Add soy sauce mixture and baste liver until mixture just comes to simmer.

vegetables

A wide range of Chinese vegetables and fruits are available in Chinese-populated communities. They are of fine quality, reasonable and garden fresh. All these produce items have very distinct differences as to flavor and texture. For instance, Chinese cabbage is markedly different than the cabbage sold in most American supermarkets. By experimenting with these vegetables in your Chinese cooking and perhaps later adding certain ones to your favorite American and European dishes, you will open up a whole new spectrum of exciting tastes and health-giving nutrition to your family.

One vegetable I'd particularly like to recommend is the bitter melon (or squash). The first thing you will notice about it is its knobby skin. When cooked—alone or with beef or chicken, etc.—it has a decidedly bitter taste. Most people quickly develop a liking for the bitter melon's unusual flavor and its cooling aftertaste. This melon, which thrives in the summertime, is very popular in South China. Because of the plant's remarkably high quinine content, the incidence of malaria in that region has been greatly curtailed.

Many markets and supermarkets today carry a limited variety of Chinese vegetables. The most easily obtainable are snow peas, bean sprouts, bok choy, Chinese cabbage, Chinese mustard greens, Chinese parsley and Chinese ginger root. My friend Jerry Baker, the American master gardener, says that many Chinese vegetables are available in seed packets and are easy and fun to grow in your garden. For information on these, write to The Perry Morse Seed Company, Mountain View, California or to the Burpee Seed Company, Philadelphia, Pennsylvania. Believe me, growing your own fresh Chinese vegetables will add immeasurably to your family's enjoyment of the recipes in this book.

I was very much surprised this past year to discover many varieties of vegetables such as fuzzy melon and bitter melon available out of season in San Francisco and Los Angeles. After a little investigation, I discovered that much of this produce is grown in Mexico and shipped to Chinatowns all over the United States.

Most of the vegetables commonly found in home vegetable gardens or at your local produce counter are readily adapted to Chinese cookery. Try some simple experiments and you'll see what I mean. For example, break or cut up some lettuce into small pieces and stir-fry. Fry it alone and you'll discover its subtle natural flavor—or simmer it with a tablespoon or two of soup stock to enhance its aroma and palatability.

Be a little adventurous with your favorite vegetables and with those included in the recipes in this section. You'll be pleased to discover and appreciate the simple but delicate aromas, textures and tastes these vegetable dishes can provide.

BASIC STIR-FRIED VEGETABLES
(Serves 4)

    3/4 lb. vegetable of your choice, washed and cut as per instructions below for each specific vegetable
    2 tablespoons oil
    1/4 teaspoon salt
    1 clove garlic, minced
    1 1/4-inch slice fresh ginger root, minced
    1 teaspoon cornstarch
    2 tablespoons water

Heat oil in *wok*, or skillet. Add salt, or garlic, or ginger and stir-fry a few seconds. Add desired vegetable and stir-fry to mix. Cover and cook a few minutes. Stir occasionally. Add a little water, if necessary, to prevent scorching. Blend cornstarch and water. Add cornstarch mixture. Stir-fry slowly until sauce thickens.

SPINACH

2 large bunches spinach, washed and drained—include leaf stems
2 cakes bean cake
1 teaspoon sugar

Follow basic recipe. Stir-fry with garlic or ginger until wilted. Add 2 cakes preserved bean cake and 1 teaspoon sugar to cornstarch mixture.

CHINESE CHARD

1 lb. Chinese chard

Follow basic recipe. Wash chard and shred leaves coarsely. Cut white part lengthwise into strips 1/2 x 2-inches or diagonally into 1/4-inch slices. Stir-fry with garlic or ginger for 2 minutes.

CAULIFLOWER

1 medium cauliflower

Follow basic recipe. Cut cauliflower into bite-size pieces. Parboil with 1 clove garlic until just tender. Drain. Stir-fry with garlic or black bean mixture, or both.

BLACK BEAN MIXTURE

1 tablespoon black beans, soaked 5 minutes and drained
1 clove garlic, minced
1 1/4-inch slice fresh ginger root, minced

Put all ingredients into bowl and mix well.

BROCCOLI

1 lb. broccoli

Follow basic recipe. Wash, drain and cut broccoli into 2-inch lengths, Separate blossoms. Peel off fibrous outer portion of stems and cut stems into pieces 2 x 1/2-inch. Stir-fry with garlic or ginger, or both. Can add 2 teaspoons wine and 1 teaspoon sugar to cornstarch mixture. Cook 3 minutes.

ASPARAGUS

1 lb. asparagus

Follow basic recipe. Cut tender portion of spears diagonally leaving tips whole. Stir-fry with garlic and/or black bean mixture. Cook 3 minutes.

CHINESE LONG BEANS

3/4 lb. Chinese long beans, tips removed and cut into 2-inch lengths
1 medium onion, peeled and finely sliced

Follow basic recipe. Use either black bean mixture, or 2 teaspoons fermented bean cake and 1 teaspoon sugar with cornstarch mixture. Cook 3 minutes.

FRENCH-CUT STRING BEANS

1 package frozen or 1 lb. fresh french-cut string beans
2 Chinese mushrooms, presoaked 20 minutes and sliced—use soaking liquid for cornstarch mixture
1 teaspoon oyster sauce
1/4 teaspoon sugar

Follow basic recipe. Add the oyster sauce and sugar to cornstarch mixture. Stir-fry with garlic. (You may substitute black bean mixture for the oyster sauce, or 1 tablespoon fermented bean cake.)

Vegetables

BEAN SPROUTS

3/4 lb. bean sprouts
1/4 cup diagonally sliced celery stalks
1/4 cup sliced carrots, parboiled—use liquid for cornstarch mixture
1/4 cup sliced bamboo shoots
1 teaspoon soy sauce—add to cornstarch mixture

Follow basic recipe. Stir-fry with ginger, celery, carrots and bamboo shoots 1 minute. Then add bean sprouts. Cook 1 minute.

CHINESE CABBAGE

1 lb. Chinese cabbage, washed and drained

Follow basic recipe. Cut cabbage into 2-inch square chunks. Stir-fry with garlic and ginger. You may add 1 tablespoon fermented bean curd and 1 teaspoon sugar to cornstarch mixture. Simmer 4 minutes.

ZUCCHINI

1 lb. zucchini
1 teaspoon soy sauce
1/2 teaspoon sugar

Follow basic recipe. Wash, scrub lightly, and cut off zucchini ends. Then cut diagonally into 1/4-inch thick slices or quarter lengthwise and cut into 1-inch chunks. Add sugar and soy sauce to cornstarch mixture. Simmer for 3 minutes.

MUSTARD GREENS

1 lb. mustard greens

Follow basic recipe. Wash and drain mustard greens. Cut into 2-inch chunks. Stir-fry with ginger or add 1 tablespoon fermented bean cake and 1/4 teaspoon sugar to cornstarch mixture. Simmer 3 minutes.

CHINESE OKRA

1 lb. Chinese okra

Follow basic recipe. Wash okra and trim ends. Halve larger portion lengthwise, then peel off ridges and cut into triangular chunks. You may add 1 teaspoon wine, 1 teaspoon soy sauce and 1/2 teaspoon sugar to cornstarch mixture. Simmer 3 minutes.

LOTUS ROOT

3/4 lb. lotus root
1 stalk celery, sliced diagonally
1 small onion, sliced
4 Chinese mushrooms, presoaked in warm water 20 minutes, drained and sliced—save water for sauce
1 teaspoon soy sauce
1/2 teaspoon sugar

Combine 1 tablespoon mushroom soaking liquid with cornstarch, soy sauce and sugar. Follow basic recipe. Wash root, halve lengthwise, then cut into 1/8-inch slices. Stir-fry vegetables with ginger and garlic. Simmer, leaving lotus root still crisp.

FUZZY MELON

1 lb. fuzzy melon

Follow basic recipe. Peel melon, rinse, and cut lengthwise into halves or quarters if large. Then cut across into 1/8-inch slices. For variation, cut lengthwise into 1/4-inch slabs, then into 1/4-inch sticks, then across into 2-inch long sticks. Stir-fry with ginger or garlic or black bean mixture. Simmer 3 minutes.

Vegetables

EGGPLANT

Follow basic recipe. Wash, peel and quarter eggplant lengthwise, then crosswise into 1/4-inch slices. Stir-fry with ginger and or garlic or black bean mixture. Simmer 3 minutes.

CHINESE SNOW PEAS

1/2 lb. Chinese snow peas, strung, washed and drained—if large, halve diagonally
2 teaspoons soy sauce
1 teaspoon sugar
1 teaspoon rice wine *or* sherry
1 tablespoon cornstarch
2 tablespoons oil
1/2 teaspoon salt
1 1/4-inch slice ginger root, minced
3/4 cup celery slices, 1/8-inch, cut diagonally
1 medium onion, peeled, halved and thinly sliced
4 dried Chinese mushrooms, presoaked 20 minutes in warm water, drained and thinly sliced—*Save liquid*

Combine soy sauce, sugar and wine. Combine cornstarch with 1/4 cup mushroom liquid. In *wok*, or skillet, heat the oil. Add salt, ginger and stir-fry a few seconds. Add celery, onion, mushrooms and stir-fry. Then cover and simmer 30 seconds. Add Chinese snow peas to the *wok* and mix. Add wine mixture and cook slowly until liquid simmers. Cover and cook 1 minute. Add cornstarch mixture and stir until sauce thickens.

Variations

One or all of the following, making adjustments in quantities of ingredients used, can be substituted or added.

Carrots—washed, sliced diagonally 1/8-inch thick. Follow above recipe, add to *wok* with celery.

Water chestnuts—peeled, washed and sliced. Follow above recipe, add to *wok* with celery.

Bamboo shoots—sliced. Follow above recipe, add to *wok* with celery.

Bean sprouts—washed and drained. Follow above recipe, add to *wok* immediately after snow peas.

Cloud's Ear Fungus—substitute 1/4 cup for mushrooms. Presoak in 1 cup cold water with 1 tablespoon oil and 1 tablespoon salt. Wash, rinse, and drain. In dry *wok*, or skillet, stir-fry until dry and crispy on medium heat. Follow snow peas recipe. Add to *wok* after adding snow peas.

seafood

When I think of seafood, nothing is more vivid in my mind than the beautiful displays of fish and shellfish neatly arranged on the marble-topped counters in the fish markets of San Franciso's Chinatown when I was very young. Even the "fishy" odors that identified the location of these shops from half a block away, gave them a certain character that was unique. The prawns, crayfish, crabs, abalone, sea bass, tuna, barracuda, smelt and squid were just a few of the varieties of seafood available in those days. I suppose the fishermen brought everything they caught in their nets down to Chinatown. It's been said that the Chinese can find a way to cook anything.

So, it was in San Francisco's Chinatown—next to the Italian section of North Beach, an area abounding with fishermen—that I learned to appreciate these whole, live or pot-ready creatures from the sea. Fish and rice was a favorite family meal—one which my father selected, prepared, cooked and set on our dining table. The menu consisted of a bowl of soup, a bowl of rice and a whole steamed fish on a platter.

Needless to say, I learned to appreciate and thoroughly enjoy seafoods prepared in many of the countless Cantonese-style recipes. They are all distinctly appetizing because each variety of fish has a decided texture and unique flavor. All seafoods are adaptable to the simple Chinese cooking methods and are a welcome addition to any menu. Enjoy the recipes in the section that follows; then experiment by using seafood in combination with, or as a substitute for the meats called for in the recipes in other parts of the book.

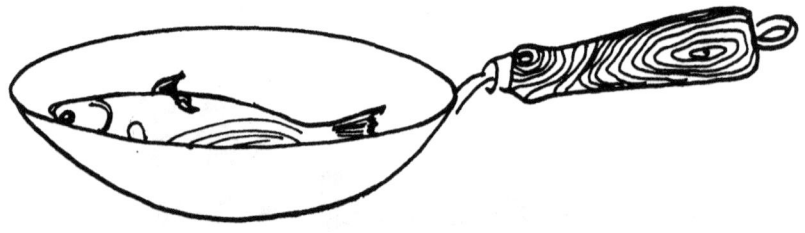

STEAMED FISH
(Serves 4 to 6)

2 lbs. sea bass *or* your favorite fresh fish, cleaned thoroughly—head and tail intact)
1 teaspoon salt
1 tablespoon soy sauce
3 tablespoons peanut oil
3 drops sesame oil
2 cloves garlic, crushed
1 tablespoon ginger, crushed
2 scallions—*white part only*—split and cut into 1-inch pieces

Rub fish with soy sauce, 1 tablespoon peanut oil, salt, 1 clove garlic. Place fish in deep dish or platter and place on rack in steamer or large kettle with about 2 to 3 inches water at bottom. (If you don't have steamer or rack, use overturned perforated coffee can as described previously.) Sprinkle ginger over fish. Cover and steam until fish is done, about 20 minutes. Heat oils in skillet, and cook the garlic for 1 minute then pour over the fish. Garnish the fish with the bacon, sweet pickles, ginger and scallions.

BRAISED FISH
(Serves 4)

1   3 lb. sea bass *or* carp
1 teaspoon salt
1/4 cup oil
2 teaspoons minced ginger root
6 scallions, sliced
1 clove garlic, minced
2 tablespoons oyster sauce
2 tablespoons soy sauce
2 teaspoons Tabasco
1 teaspoon sugar
1 cup hot chicken broth

Clean the fish and leave it whole. Rub salt into it. Heat the oil in *wok*, or skillet, and stir in the ginger, scallions, garlic, oyster sauce, soy sauce, tabasco and sugar. Cook for 1 minute. Add the fish and brown on both sides. Add the chicken broth. Cover and cook over low heat 15 minutes or until fish flakes easily with fork.

FISH AND ONIONS
(Serves 4)

1 lb. fresh swordfish, mackerel *or* tuna filet
1 teaspoon minced ginger root
2 tablespoons soy sauce
3 tablespoons oil
2 tablespoons cornstarch
2 cups sliced onions
2 tablespoons rice wine *or* sherry
1/2 cup green peas
1 tablespoon sugar
1/4 teaspoon MSG

Cut fish into 1/4-inch squares. Combine ginger and soy sauce, and marinate fish 15 minutes. Drain; keep marinade. Heat oil in *wok*, or skillet. Roll fish in cornstarch, then brown on both sides in oil. Remove. Sauté onions in remaining oil in *wok* for 3 minutes. Add wine, peas, sugar, marinade, MSG and fish. Simmer for 5 minutes.

SWEET-AND-SOUR FRIED FISH
(Serves 4 to 6)

1 3-lb. bass *or* cod
3 tablespoons finely chopped onion
3 teaspoons chopped ginger root
1 teaspoon soy sauce
2 teaspoons salt
1/3 teaspoon MSG
1 teaspoon rice wine *or* sherry
1/8 teaspoon pepper
1/2 cup cornstarch
Peanut oil for deep frying
3/4 cup cider vinegar
1/4 cup sugar
3 scallions, sliced
1 green *or* red pepper, shredded
1 carrot, shredded
2 tablespoons Chinese preserved sweet pickles, thinly sliced *or* substitute American sweet pickles

Split the fish and bone. Leave head and tail intact, if desired. Combine with onions, 1 teaspoon ginger, soy sauce, 1 teaspoon salt, MSG, wine and pepper. Rub into fish and let stand for 30 minutes. Roll the fish in the cornstarch and let stand 5 minutes. In *wok*, or skillet, heat the peanut oil to 350° and fry the fish in it for 15 minutes. Drain the fish and cover with the following sauce mixture by mixing together the vinegar, 1 tablespoon cornstarch, scallions, pepper, carrot, pickles, remaining ginger and salt. Cook over low heat, stirring until sauce thickens.

ALMOND FRIED FISH
(Serves 4)

3 pieces sole filet
2 teaspoons grated onion
1/2 teaspoon powdered ginger
1 teaspoon salt
1 teaspoon sugar
1 teaspoon cornstarch
2 teaspoons soy sauce
1 teaspoon rice wine *or* sherry
1 egg, beaten
3/4 cup ground almonds
3 slices ham, cut in 2-inch strips
3 tablespoons oil

Cut sole in 1/2 lengthwise, then crosswise, about 2-inch x 3-inch pieces. Mix together the onions, ginger, salt, sugar, cornstarch, soy sauce, wine and eggs. Dip the fish pieces in the mixture, then dip one side in the almonds. Roll the fish—almond side in—around the ham strips. Heat the oil in *wok*, or skillet, and fry the fish until browned.

ORIENTAL FISH CAKES
(Serves 4)

1/2 lb. raw shrimp, shelled and deveined
1 lb. pike *or* flounder filet
1 cup blanched almonds
2 slices bacon
1 teaspoon salt
1 tablespoon soy sauce
1 tablespoon cornstarch
3/4 cup oil

Chop together the shrimp, fish, almonds and bacon. Blend in salt, soy sauce, cornstarch and 1 tablespoon oil. Shape the mixture into flat patties, using two tablespoons mixture for each. Heat the remaining oil in *wok*, or skillet, and fry the patties until browned on both sides.

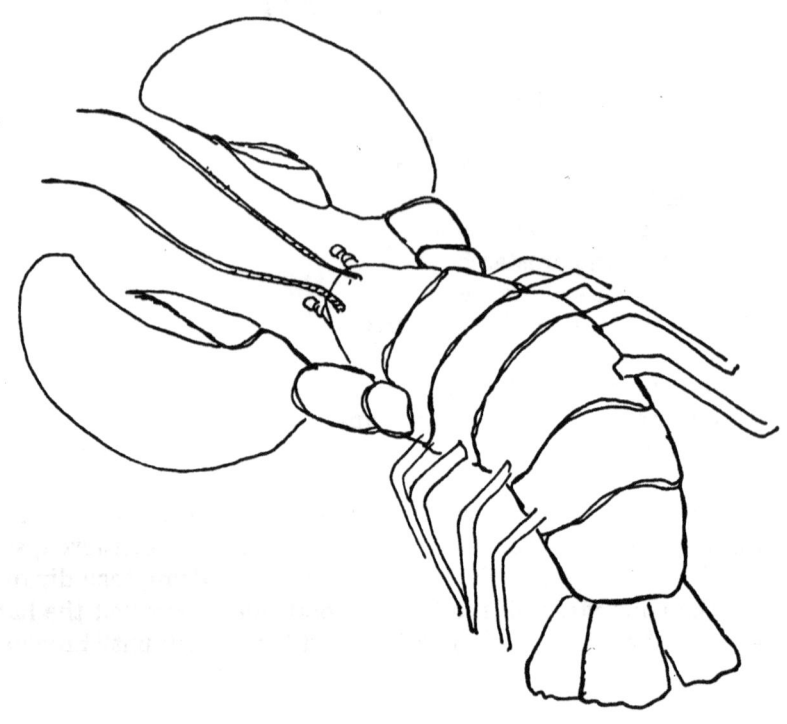

STEAMED LOBSTER
(Serves 4)

    1 2-lb. lobster
    1/2 teaspoon salt
    1/3 teaspoon MSG
    Pinch garlic salt
    Dash pepper
    2 tablespoons rice wine *or* sherry
    1 teaspoon crushed ginger root
    1 teaspoon soy sauce
    2 tablespoons peanut oil
    1/8 teaspoon sesame seed oil

Clean and split lobster in half. Split claws and place in serving dish, shellside down. Combine salt, MSG, garlic salt, pepper, wine, ginger root and soy sauce, and pour over lobster. Steam for 15 minutes. Heat peanut oil and sesame oil together in *wok* and pour over lobster. Serve hot.

STIR-FRIED LOBSTER WITH VEGETABLES AND ALMONDS
(Serves 4 to 6)

1-1/2 lbs. cooked lobster meat, diced
2 teaspoons soy sauce
2 tablespoons rice wine *or* sherry
1/3 teaspoon ginger powder
1/2 tablespoon water
1 tablespoon cornstarch
1 cup water
Dash of pepper
1 teaspoon sugar
1/3 teaspoon MSG
1 tablespoon peanut oil
1 teaspoon salt
1 clove garlic, crushed
1 cup Chinese black mushrooms—or white—if dried, presoak 15 minutes, drain and dice
1/4 cup diced celery
1/4 cup diced onion
1/4 cup bamboo shoots
1/4 cup peeled and diced water chestnuts
1/4 cup soup stock
1/3 cup crushed roasted almonds
1/4 cup fresh peas, cooked 2 minutes *or* frozen, thawed
1/2 cup peapods—*optional*

Combine 1 teaspoon soy sauce, wine, ginger and 1 tablespoon water. Combine cornstarch, and pepper with sugar, MSG, 1 teaspoon soy sauce and 1/2 cup water. Heat peanut oil in *wok*, or skillet and add salt and garlic. Add mushrooms, celery, onion, bamboo shoots and water chestnuts. Stir-fry about 2 minutes. Add lobster meat and stir-fry 1 minute. To this add wine mixture and cook for 1 minute. Add soup stock. Cover and simmer 3 minutes. Add cornstarch combination and cook until sauce thickens and is smooth. Serve hot with boiled rice. Garnish with almonds and peas.

FRIED LOBSTER IN BLACK BEAN SAUCE
(Serves 4 to 6)

1 2-lb. lobster
1/4 lb. pork, chopped
1 tablespoon black bean sauce, washed and mashed
2 cloves garlic, crushed
Dash pepper
5 tablespoons water
2 teaspoons soy sauce
1 teaspoon rice wine *or* sherry
1 teaspoon shredded ginger root
1 teaspoon sugar
1/2 teaspoon MSG
1 tablespoon cornstarch
1/2 cup water
1 tablespoon peanut oil
1/2 teaspoon salt
1/2 cup soup stock
1 egg, beaten
1/2 scallion, chopped

Combine bean sauce, garlic and pepper with 1 tablespoon water. Combine soy sauce, wine, ginger root, sugar and 4 tablespoons water. Combine MSG, cornstarch and 1/2 cup water. Cut the lobster in half through the shell, then crosswise. Crack claws. Cut meat areas into 1-inch pieces. Heat peanut oil in *wok*, or skillet, and add salt. Then add bean sauce combination and stir-fry 1/2 minute. Add pork and lobster, and stir-fry 2 minutes or until golden brown. Add soup stock. Cover and simmer 5 minutes. Then add beaten egg and chopped scallion. Stir-fry 1/2 minute and add cornstarch combination. Simmer until sauce thickens. Serve hot with rice.

SHRIMP CHOP SUEY
(Serves 4)

3/4 lb. shrimp, cleaned and deveined
2 tablespoons cornstarch
2 tablespoons soy sauce

1/4 cup water
2 tablespoons peanut oil
1 teaspoon salt
1/4 teaspoon black pepper
1 large onion, cut in 8 wedges
3 stalks celery, cut diagonally in 1/4-inch pieces
1/4 cup hot beef broth (or chicken)
1 10-oz. can bean sprouts *or* 1/2 lb. fresh bean sprouts

Combine cornstarch, soy sauce and water and blend well. Heat oil in *wok*, or skillet, with salt and pepper. Add the shrimp and stir-fry 5 minutes or until pink. Remove. Add onion wedges and celery pieces, and stir-fry over medium heat for a few seconds. Add the beef broth and simmer covered over low heat for 5 minutes. Add bean sprouts. Cook 3 minutes. Return the shrimp and add the cornstarch mixture. Stir and simmer until sauce thickens.

CRAB MEAT WITH PORK
(Serves 4)

1 lb. crab meat
1/4 lb. pork, minced
3 tablespoons oil
2 eggs, beaten
2 tablespoons soy sauce
1 tablespoon rice wine *or* sherry
1 teaspoon salt
1/2 teaspoon sugar
2 tablespoons water
3 scallions, chopped

Heat the oil in *wok*, or skillet, and sauté the pork for 5 minutes. Stir in the eggs and then add the soy sauce, wine, salt, sugar, water and crab meat. Mix well and cook over low heat 4 minutes. Garnish with scallions.

STIR-FRIED ABALONE SLICES WITH BLACK MUSHROOMS
(Serves 4)

1 15-oz. can abalone—*save liquid*
1 tablespoon cornstarch
2 tablespoons abalone liquid
2 tablespoons oil
1/2 teaspoon salt
1/4 cup dried black mushrooms, presoaked and sliced
1/2 cup sliced bamboo shoots
1/3 cup abalone liquid
1 green onion, chopped

Cut abalone lengthwise and slice across into 1/8-inch slices. Combine cornstarch and 2 tablespoons abalone liquid. In *wok*, or skillet, heat oil and add salt. Then add mushrooms and bamboo shoots. Stir-fry to mix. Add 1/3 cup abalone liquid and bring to a boil. Reduce heat, simmer 3 minutes. Add abalone slices and stir-fry 30 seconds. Add cornstarch mixture and cook until sauce thickens. Garnish with green onions.

STIR-FRIED ABALONE SLICES WITH OYSTER SAUCE
(Serves 4)

1-lb. can abalone
1/2 cup abalone liquid—from can
1 tablespoon cornstarch
3 tablespoons oyster sauce
1 tablespoon soy sauce
2 tablespoons oil
1 1/4-inch slice ginger root, minced
1 green onion, finely chopped

Cut abalone lengthwise and slice crosswise into 1/8-inch slices. Combine abalone liquid with cornstarch and mix in oyster and soy sauces. In *wok*, or skillet, heat oil and add ginger. Stir-fry a few seconds and then add abalone slices. Stir-fry 30 seconds. Add cornstarch mixture and cook until sauce thickens. Serve on platter and garnish with green onions.

DICED ABALONE WITH VEGETABLES
(Serves 4)

1-lb. can abalone—*save liquid*
2 tablespoons abalone liquid
1 tablespoon cornstarch
2 tablespoons oyster sauce
2 tablespoons oil
1/2 teaspoon salt
1 1/4-inch slice ginger root, minced
1/4 cup dried Chinese mushrooms, presoaked and diced
1/4 cup peeled and diced water chestnuts
1/4 cup diced bamboo shoots
1 green onion, chopped
1/2 cup green peas—if fresh, blanched
1/3 cup abalone liquid
1 teaspoon soy sauce

Dice abalone and set aside. Combine 2 tablespoons abalone liquid with cornstarch and oyster sauce. Heat oil in *wok*, or skillet, and add salt and ginger. Add vegetables and stir-fry few seconds to mix. Add 1/3 cup abalone liquid and the soy sauce, and bring to active simmer. Cover and cook 3 minutes. Add abalone and stir-fry 30 seconds. Stir in cornstarch-abalone-liquid mixture and simmer until sauce thickens.

OYSTER RICE
(Serves 4)

1 pint oysters, drained
2 cups rice
1-3/4 cups water
1/4 cup soy sauce
1-1/2 teaspoons MSG
1/4 cup rice wine

Wash rice and add water. Let stand for 1 hour. Cut oysters into 3 parts. Add oyster, soy sauce, MSG and sake to rice, and cook in manner described in the rice section of book.

STIR-FRIED FRESH SQUID
(Serves 4)

1-lb. fresh squid
2 tablespoons soup stock *or* water
1 teaspoon cornstarch
1/4 teaspoon MSG
2 tablespoons oil
1 1/4-inch slice ginger root, minced
1/2 teaspoon salt
2 scallions, split lengthwise and cut into 1-1/8-inch lengths
1 tablespoon soy sauce
1 tablespoon rice wine *or* sherry

Clean squid; trim and discard tentacles; score and cut into 1-1/2-inch squares. Combine soup stock, cornstarch and MSG. Heat oil in *wok*, or skillet, and add the ginger, salt and scallions. Stir-fry few seconds. Add squid and stir-fry 1 minute. Add the soy sauce and wine. Stir-fry 2 minutes. Add soup stock-cornstarch mixture and cook until sauce thickens.

noodles 麵

At Chinese banquets, particularly birthday celebrations, noodles are served as a last course. This is done in appreciation of a good life and hopeful anticipation of a long one. Noodles can be boiled, steamed, panfried and deep fried. Fresh noodles can be purchased like won ton wrappings and by the pound. The great advantage of noodle dishes is the ready availability of packaged dry noodles and easy substitution of other types of pasta.

Making Noodles

Noodles can be made following the recipe for won ton wrappings, except that the rolled-out sheets are cut into 8-inch-wide strips, stacked and then cut crosswise into fine threads.

Boiled Noodles

Immerse noodles in actively boiling salted water for about 3 minutes. Drain in colander; then rinse in cold water. This halts the cooking process and also washes away excess starch so that the noodles do not become matted together. Dropping a tablespoon of oil into the boiling water adds to the texture and helps keep the frothing water from boiling over. Reheat by immersing in boiling water and draining. I'm lazy, so I run it under the hot water tap.

Panfried Noodles

In *wok*, or skillet, heat about 1/4-inch oil in bottom of pan. Drop enough cooked noodles into pan so that they are spread evenly on bottom of pan for even browning. When crisp, golden brown, turn noodle pancake over and brown other side. Noodles absorb oil, so more oil should be added as needed in the frying process. Pan-fried noodles can be kept in a warming oven until ready for use.

Deep-Fried Noodles

In hot *wok*, or skillet, drop uncooked fresh noodles into the deep hot oil and cook, stirring occasionally, until golden brown. Be careful not to put too much into the pan at one time, because the noodles have a tendency to puff up. These are the crispy noodles usually served in Chinese restaurants. They are also available commercially in vacuum-packed tins. By the way, they're wonderful as a snack or as nibbling food with beer or cocktails.

Yut Gaw Min

Yut gaw min is usually the waiter's call into the chef. Literally, it means one each noodle. The Japanese have something similar in *saimin* (little noodle). The American customer who picks up a menu and is desirous of this nourishing dish will point to the menu or request "pork noodles." For the home, this is a quick hot meal in which tidbits of meat and chopped scallions can be used to garnish this bowl of cooked noodles in hot broth. Noodles in Soup is simply that: noodles, soup and garnish.

Chow Mein

There has been some confusion between chop suey, chow yuk and chow mein. Chop suey has become the general term for Chinese food, which literally means *cut up pieces*. Chow yuk is a general term for stir-fried meat dishes. Chow mein is the identifying term for noodles stir-fried with other ingredients. One could easily say chow mein is chow yuk with noodles instead of rice.

Chow mein is served two ways: with noodles on the bottom of the platter and topped with stir-fried ingredients, or with noodles stir-fried and mixed with all the ingredients (lo mein).

So, to your own tastes, you can prepare suitable, delightful dishes of chow mein. I really "mein" it!

PORK WITH NOODLES (LO-MEIN)
(Serves 4)

1 lb. pork, cut into thin strips
1-1/2 tablespoons cornstarch
3/4 cup chicken broth
1 tablespoon peanut oil
1 teaspoon salt
1/4 teaspoon black pepper
2 cups bean sprouts
1/2 cup sliced celery
1/2 cup sliced Chinese cabbage
2 tablespoons soy sauce
1 teaspoon sugar
3 cups fine noodles, cooked and drained
1/4 cup chopped green onion

Mix cornstarch and chicken broth together well. Heat peanut oil in *wok*, or skillet. Stir-fry pork until browned. Add salt, pepper, bean sprouts, celery, Chinese cabbage, soy sauce and sugar. Cover and simmer 5 minutes. Add noodles and stir in thoroughly. Add chicken-broth mixture and cook until gravy thickens. Place on platter and garnish with green onions.

PORK CHOW MEIN
(Serves 4)

1/2 lb. lean pork
1 tablespoon cornstarch
2 tablespoons soy sauce
Dash black pepper
1/2 teaspoon salt
1/2 teaspoon sugar
1 teaspoon rice wine *or* sherry
3/4 cup water
Oil for frying
1 egg, beaten
1 lb. egg noodles
Peanut oil for frying noodles
1 tablespoon vegetable oil
2 large dried Chinese mushrooms, presoaked and sliced
2 stalks celery, sliced diagonally
1/2 large onion, sliced
1/2 lb. fresh bean sprouts *or* 1/2 lb. Chinese cabbage
1/2 cup Chinese pea pods, stringed and cut in halves
2-3 scallions, chopped

Cut pork across grain into small pieces. Marinate pork in mixture of cornstarch, 1 tablespoon soy sauce, pepper, salt, sugar and wine approximately 15 minutes. Save marinade. Mix with 1/2 cup water and the remaining tablespoon of soy sauce and set aside. Fry the beaten egg in *wok*, or skillet, in form of very thin pancake. Remove, cool and then slice into 2-inch strips. Slice across into fine, smaller Julienne strips. Set aside. Cook noodles in boiling water for 3 minutes. Rinse with cold water and let drain until thoroughly dry. Fry the noodles, a small portion at a time, in oil until gold in color. Place in 250° oven. Pour vegetable oil in *wok*, or skillet, and stir-fry pork and mushrooms on high flame until pork is browned. Remove to dish or bowl. Add the celery and onion to *wok* and stir-fry 2 minutes. Then add bean sprouts and Chinese peas, and stir-fry for 1 minute. Return the pork and mushroom mixture to *wok*. Pour the cornstarch mixture used as marinade into *wok* and stir. Cook until gravy thickens. Place panfried noodles on platter. Pour pork-and-vegetable mixture over noodles, and garnish with chopped green onion and egg strips.

index

abalone 20
abalone and chicken soup 95
abalone with pickled scallions 65
abalone with pork balls 96
almond fried fish 199
appetizers
  abalone with pickled scallions 65
  bacon-wrapped water chestnuts 59
  bar-b-cued spareribs 61
  beef balls 57
  beef jerky 61
  broiled chicken with giblets 62
  broiled clams 67
  chicken wings stewed in wine
    sauce 71
  crab puffs 68
  deep-fried fish cakes 70
  eggs stuffed with crab 66
  fish rolls 70
  foil-wrapped chicken 68
  marinated abalone cubes 69
  marinated beef chunks 57
  marinated mushroom caps 63
  meatballs in mushroom sauce 63
  oyster fritters 64
  pork balls 56
  pork and crab meat balls 65
  rolled beef bits 64
  rumaki 58
  scallops in wine sauce 62
  shrimp balls 56
  shrimp delight 67
  shrimp toast 69
  spicy chicken livers 66
  steamed Chinese pork sausage 58
  stuffed mushrooms 59
anise 20
asparagus 190

bacon-wrapped water chestnuts 59
bar-b-cued spareribs 61
barbecued pork 60
basic soups 74-75
   chicken 74
   minced pork 75
   pork 75
   variations of basic soups 75-79
basic steamed eggs 111
basic steamed sliced beef 166
basic steamed pork 116
basic stir-fried vegetables 188
bean curd 20
bean sprouts 191
bean threads 20
beef 61, 63, 64, 163-185
   basic steamed sliced beef 166
   beef balls roasted in wine sauce 165
   beef with asparagus 168
   beef balls 57
   beef balls roasted in wine sauce 165
   beef with fresh bean curd 169
   beef with bean sprouts 170
   beef with bell peppers 171
   beef with bitter melon 172
   beef with bitter melon and black bean sauce 173
   beef with broccoli 173
   beef with cauliflower 175
   beef with Chinese broccoli 174
   beef with Chinese chard 176
   beef with Chinese long beans 177
   beef with Chinese turnips 178
   beef chop suey 181
   beef with curry 182
   beef with ginger 183
   beef in gravy sauce 182
   beef with French-cut string beans 178
   beef with fresh bean curd 169
   beef with fresh mushrooms 172

beef jerky 61
beef soup and Chinese turnips 88
beef with string beans 177
beef with tomatoes 171
beef and snow peas 178
bird's nest 21
bitter melon (squash) 187
black bean mixture 189
black bean sauce 168
black mushroom duck soup 84
black mushrooms 23
boiled chicken with giblets 62
boiled beef tongue 184
braised beef chunks 164
braised fish 197
braised pork shoulder 114
braised pork and spinach 132
braised pork with spinach 133
broccoli 190
broccoli with braised pork 126
broiled chicken with giblets 62
broiled clams 67
broiled ginger steak 164

Cantonese fried chicken 150
Cantonese style 150, 151
cauliflower 175, 189
chicken 58, 62, 66, 68, 71, 141-162
   boiled with giblets 62
   Cantonese fried chicken 150
   chicken with almonds 148
   chicken with almonds and mushrooms 142
   chicken with almonds and water chestnuts 142
   chicken and bell peppers 143
   chicken and black mushrooms 144
   chicken and button mushrooms 145
   chicken and cashews 148
   chicken and chestnuts 145

Index

chicken and ham and broccoli 146
chicken with pineapple 146
chicken puffs 160
chicken pot roast 155
chicken roasted with tangerine peel 156
chicken and tomatoes 147
chicken and walnuts 148
chicken wings stewed in wine sauce 71
Chinese chicken salad-one 161
Chinese chicken salad-two 162
curried chicken 158
deep-fried chicken in batter with vegetables 154
fried boneless chicken Cantonese 151
fried chicken-Chinese style 150
soy chicken 159
spiced roast chicken 156
spicy Szechwan chicken with tangerine peel 149
steamed soy sauce chicken 159
stir-fried curled chicken with lichee 153
stir-fried curled chicken with vegetables 152
sweet-and-sour chicken 157
chicken with almonds 148
chicken with almonds and water chestnuts 142
chicken and bell peppers 143
chicken and black mushrooms 144
chicken and button mushrooms 145
chicken and cashews 148
chicken and chestnuts 145
chicken with pineapple 146
chicken soups 80-83
  and barley 80
  dried fungus and 83
  and egg flower 80
  giblet 81
  with mixed vegetables 82
  with noodles 81
  and peas 82
chicken and tomatoes 147
chicken and walnuts 148
Chinese barbecued pork 121
Chinese cabbage 187, 191
Chinese cabbage soup 86
Chinese chard 189
Chinese chicken salad-one 161
Chinese chicken salad-two 162
Chinese foods 11-29, 30-44, 50-71, 73-101, 103-112, 187-211
  appetizers 55-71
  beef 163-185
  Cantonese style 5, 150, 151
  chicken 141-162
  chow mein 207-210
  condiments 19-25
  eggs 103-112
  groceries 26-27
  mail-order list 211
  pork 113-140
  preparing and cooking 39-40
  rice 41-44
  sauces 27-28
  Shanghai-style 5
  shopping 11-12, 211
  soups 73-101
  Szechwan style 5, 98, 140
  tea 28-30
  utensils 33-38
  vegetables 13-17, 59, 63, 187-194
    American substitutes for Chinese 18-19
  wines 30-31
  won ton 50-54
Chinese long beans 190
Chinese okra 192
Chinese sausage 21

Chinese snow peas 193
  variations 193-194
    bamboo shoots 194
    bean sprouts 194
    carrots 193
    clouds' ear fungus 194
    water chestnuts 194
chopsticks 36-37
  Chinese 37
  cooking 37, 38
  description 37
  history 36
  Japanese 37
  use 37
chop suey 5
  pork chop suey 121
chow mein 207-210
clam and beef soup 94
clear fresh bean curd 86
clear watercress soup 89
clouds' ear fungus 21
cornstarch 26
crab meat with pork 203
crab puffs 68
crackling rice 43
crisp eggs with oyster sauce 111
curried chicken 158
curry powder 26
cuttlefish 22

deep-fried chicken in batter with vegetables 154
deep-fried eggs with oyster sauce 111
deep-fried fish cakes 70
deep-fried pork balls with lettuce 139
deep-fried pork with mixed vegetables 138
diced abalone with vegetables 205
diced chicken giblets and pork 120
dried Chinese cabbage 21
dried Chinese chard soup 87

dried fungus and chicken soup 83
dried lily buds (gold needles) 23
dried lily soup with mixed meats 84
dried oyster and bean curd soup 96
dried oysters 23
dried shrimp 24
dried tangerine peel 25

egg foo yung, basic recipe 107
egg foo yung sauce 108
egg foo yung, variations 108
  barbecued pork 108
  chicken and bean sprouts 109
  chicken and fresh mushrooms 109
  clams 108
  cooked ham 109
  crab 109
  shrimp 108
  turkey meat 109
  vegetables only 109
eggplant 193
eggplant and pork 128
egg rolls 47-50
  deep fried 50
  fillings 48
  pan fried 50
  shaping 49
  skins 48
  steamed 50
eggs 47-50, 60, 66, 103, 112
  basic recipe for egg foo yung 107
  basic recipe for stir-fried eggs 104
  basic steamed eggs 111
  crisp eggs with oyster sauce 111
  deep-fried eggs with oyster sauce 111
  egg foo yung sauce 108
  egg rolls 47-50
  stir-fried eggs with pork and mushrooms 104
  three varieties of steamed eggs 105
  variations for egg foo yung 108

Index

variations for steamed eggs 112
variations for stir-fried eggs 104
egg strainer 38
eggs stuffed with crab 66

fermented bean curd 20
fish ball soup 91
fish and onions 197
fish and vegetable soup 91
fish rolls 70
foil-wrapped chicken 68
foo jook 24
French-cut string beans 190
fresh bean curd and cabbage soup 87
fresh ham Hong Kong 115
fried boneless chicken Cantonese 151
fried chicken-Chinese-style 150
fried lobster in black bean sauce 202
fried rice, basic 44
fuzzy melon 192

garlic 25
grass mushrooms 23
green peppers stuffed with pork 130
ground pork with green beans 129

ham and vegetable soup 99
ham-cured smoked pork 26
Hong Kong sauce 115
hot pork and chicken with vegetables 119
hot and sour soup Szechwan 98
hoy sin sauce 27

kitchen tools 38
   chopsticks 37, 38
   egg strainer 38
   scoop 38
   spatula 38
   strainer 38
   wok brush 38

lobster and watercress soup 88
lo-mein 209
lotus root 192
lotus root soup 88

marinated abalone cubes 69
marinated beef chunks 57
marinated mushroom caps 63
meatballs in mushroom sauce 63
methods of cooking 39-40
   barbecuing 40
   boiling 40
   braising 40
   deep frying 39
   double-boiling in steam 39
   red-stewing 39
   steaming 39
   stir-frying 39
methods of preparation 39-40
monosodium glutamate 26
mustard 26
mustard greens 191
mustard green soup 85
noodles 207-210
   boiled 207
   deep-fried 208
   lo-mein 209
   making noodles 207
   pan-fried 208
   pork with noodles 209
   yut gaw min 208

oil 26
Oriental fish cakes 199
oyster fritters 64
oyster rice 205
oyster sauce 23, 111

parsley clam soup 94
pickled scallions 24

pork 56, 58, 59, 60, 61, 65, 113-140
  bacon-wrapped water chestnuts 59
  balls 56
  bar-b-cued spareribs 61
  barbecued pork 60
  basic steamed 116
  braised pork shoulder 114
  braised pork and spinach 132
  braised pork with spinach 133
  broccoli with braised pork 126
  Chinese barbecued pork 121
  deep-fried pork balls with lettuce 139
  deep-fried pork with mixed vegetables 138
  diced chicken giblets and pork 120
  eggplant and pork 128
  fresh ham Hong Kong 115
  green peppers stuffed with pork 130
  ground pork with green beans 129
  Hong Kong sauce 115
  hot pork and chicken with vegetables 119
  pork balls 56
  pork with bamboo shoots 124
  pork with broccoli and vermicelli 126
  pork with Chinese long beans and water chestnuts 131
  pork chops Cathay 137
  pork chops with oyster sauce 137
  pork chop suey 121
  pork and crab meat balls 65
  pork with fresh bean curd 125
  pork with green beans 129
  pork with green peppers 129
  pork with leeks and pineapple 130
  pork with peapods and turnips 132
  pork spareribs in black bean sauce 122-123
  pork with vegetables 124
  pork and water chestnuts 134
  round ham of pork with spinach 116
  spicy twice-cooked Szechwan pork 140
  steamed pork cubes 118
  steamed minced pork with ham 119
  steamed pork with salted cabbage 118
  stir-fried pork with bamboo shoots 134
  stir-fried pork with green onions 135
  stir-fried pork with onions 123
  stir-fried pork with peapods 135
  stir-fried sweet-and-sour pork in egg batter 136
  sweet-and-sour spareribs 122
  variations for steamed pork 117
pork balls 56
pork and bamboo shoots 124
pork and bean cake soup 99
pork with broccoli and vermicelli 126
pork with Chinese long beans and water chestnuts 131
pork chops Cathay 137
pork with green peppers 129
pork chops with oyster sauce 137
pork chop suey 121
pork and crab meat balls 65
pork with fresh bean curd 125
pork with green beans 129
pork with leeks and pineapple 130
pork meatball soup 97
pork with peapods and turnips 132
pork spareribs in black bean sauce 122-123
pork with vegetables 124
pork and water chestnuts 134

quick-cooked watercress soup 90

Index

red dates 24
rice 41-46
  basic fried 44
  congee 46
  cooked 42
  crackling 43
  variations 45
rice congee 46
rice wine 28
rolled beef bits 64
round ham of pork and spinach 116
rumaki 58

salt-cured turnips 22
salted black beans 24
salted duck eggs 22
sauces 27-28, 115
  black bean mixture 27
  black bean sauce 122-123
  egg foo yung sauce 108
  Hong Kong sauce 115
  hoy sin sauce 27
  oyster sauce 23, 111
  plum sauce 28
  shrimp paste 28
  soy sauce 27
seafood 40, 56, 62, 64, 65, 67, 68, 69, 195-206
  almond fried fish 199
  braised fish 197
  crab meat with pork 203
  diced abalone with vegetables 205
  fish and onions 197
  fried lobster in black bean sauce 202
  oriental fish cakes 199
  oyster rice 205
  shrimp chop suey 202
  steamed fish 196
  steamed lobster 200

  stir-fried abalone slices with black mushrooms 204
  stir-fried abalone slices with oyster sauce 204
  stir-fried fresh squid 206
  stir-fried lobster with vegetables and almonds 201
  sweet-and-sour fried fish 198
sesame oil 27
seeds 26
shark's fin soup 97
shrimp and cabbage soup 92
shrimp chop suey 202
shrimp and corn soup 93
shrimp soup 92
soups 73-101
  abalone and chicken 95
  abalone with pork balls 96
  basic soups 74-75
    chicken 74
    minced pork 75
    pork 75
  variations of basic soups 75-79
  beef with Chinese turnips 88
  black mushroom duck soup 84
  chicken soups 80-83
    and barley 80
    dried fungus and 83
    egg flower 80
    giblet soup 81
    with mixed vegetables 82
    with noodles 81
    and peas 82
    Chinese cabbage 86
  clam and beef 94
  clear fresh bean curd 86
  clear watercress 89
  dried Chinese chard 87
  dried fungus and chicken 83

dried lily with mixed meats 84
dried oyster and bean curd 96
fish and vegetable 91
fresh bean curd and cabbage 87
fish ball 91
ham and vegetable 99
hot and sour Szechwan 98
lobster and watercress 88
lotus root 88
mustard green 85
parsley clam 94
pork and bean cake 99
pork meatball 97
quick-cooked watercress 90
shark's fin 97
shrimp 92
shrimp and cabbage 92
shrimp and corn 93
spinach, clam and egg 95
spinach and egg 85
watercress 89
whole winter melon with diced meats 101
winter melon with ham and chicken soup 100
won ton 100

spinach 189
spinach, clam, and egg soup 95
spinach and egg soup 85
snow peas 187
soy chicken 159
spiced roast chicken 156
spicy chicken livers 66
spicy Szechwan chicken with tangerine peel 149
spicy twice-cooked Szechwan pork 140
shrimp delight 67
shrimp toast 69

steamed beef balls 167
steamed beef with water chestnuts 167
steamed Chinese pork sausage 58
steamed eggs, three varieties 105
steamed eggs, variations 112
steamed fish 196
steamed lobster 200
steamed pork cubes 118
steamed minced pork with ham 119
steamed pork with salted cabbage 118
steamed soy sauce chicken 159
stir-fried abalone slices with black mushrooms 204
stir-fried abalone slices with oyster sauce 204
stir-fried fresh squid 206
stir-fried beef with mushrooms and bamboo shoots 180
stir-fried calf liver 185
stir-fried curled chicken with lichee 153
stir-fried curled chicken with vegetables 152
stir-fried eggs, basic recipe 104
stir-fried eggs with pork and mushrooms 104
stir-fried eggs, variations 104
stir-fried lobster with vegetables and almonds 201
stir-fried pork with bamboo shoots 134
stir-fried pork with green onions 135
stir-fried pork with onions 123
stir-fried pork with peapods 135
stir-fried sweet-and-sour pork in egg batter 136
stuffed mushrooms 59
sweet-and-sour chicken 157
sweet-and-sour fried fish 198
sweet-and-sour spareribs 122
Szechwan style 5, 98, 140, 149

Index

tea 28-30
  black 29
  brewing 30
  green 29

utensils 33-38
  chopsticks 36-37
  cleaver 35-36
  kitchen tools 38
  wok 33-35

variations of steamed pork 117
vegetables 13-19, 59, 63, 187-194
  asparagus 190
  bamboo shoots 124
  basic stir-fried vegetables 188
  bean sprouts 109, 191
  bitter melon 187
  black bean mixture 189
  broccoli 190
  braised pork and spinach 132
  broccoli with braised pork 126
  cauliflower 175, 189
  Chinese cabbage 118, 187, 191
  Chinese chard 189
  Chinese long beans 190
  Chinese okra 192
  Chinese snow peas 193
  deep-fried pork with mixed vegetables 138
  eggplant 193
  eggplant and pork 128
  egg foo yung with vegetables only 109
  French-cut string beans 190
  fuzzy melon 192
  green peppers stuffed with pork 130
  leeks, pork and pineapple 130
  lotus root 192
  mustard greens 191

pork with bamboo shoots 124
pork with broccoli and vermicelli 126
pork with Chinese long beans and water chestnuts 131
pork with pea pods and turnips 132
snow peas 187
spinach 189
water chestnuts 131, 142
watercress 88, 89, 90
zucchini 191
watercress soup 89
whole winter melon with diced meats soup 101
wine 30-31
  in the U.S. 31
    Kaoling 31
    Mui Kwai Lo 31
    Ng Gah Pei 31
    Sooching 31
  white 31
  yellow 31
winter melon with ham and chicken soup 100
wok 33
  history 33
  types 34-35
    electric 35
    flat-bottom 34
    one-handle 34
    standard unit 34
won ton 50-54
  basic wrappings 52
  filling 52
  fried, plain 53
  fried, sweet and sour 53
  in soup 54, 100
won ton soup 100

zucchini 191

www.ingramcontent.com/pod-product-compliance
Lightning Source LLC
Chambersburg PA
CBHW070549160426
43199CB00014B/2431